The Dynamics of
Church
Finance

The Dynamics of
Church
Finance

JAMES D. BERKLEY

Baker Books

A Division of Baker Book House Co
Grand Rapids, Michigan 49516

Published by Baker Books
a division of Baker Book House Company
P.O. Box 6287, Grand Rapids, MI 49516-6287

Printed in the United States of America

Library of Congress Cataloging-in-Publication Data

Berkley, James D., 1950–
   The dynamics of church finance / James D. Berkley.
      p.   cm. — (Ministry dynamics for a new century series)
   Includes bibliographical references (p.   ) and index.
   ISBN 0-8010-9105-5 (paper)
   1. Church finance. I. Title. II. Ministry dynamics for a new century.
BV770.B475   2000
254'.8—dc21   00-041465

For current information about all releases from Baker Book House, visit our web site:

http://www.bakerbooks.com

To my mother,
Erma Van Meter Berkley,
in whose home I first learned stewardship
and responsibility,
and to whose gracious home I retreated
to write this book

Contents

Series Preface

The purpose of the Ministry Dynamics series is to provide both experienced and beginning pastors with concise information that will help them do the task of ministry with efficiency, fruitfulness, and joy.

The word *ministry* means "service," something that Jesus exemplified in his own life and that he expects us to practice in our lives. No matter what our title or position, we are in the church to serve God's people. The word *dynamics* is not used as an equivalent of "power" but as a reminder that nothing stands still in Christian ministry. If it does, it dies. True biblical ministry involves constant challenge and change, learning and growth, and how we handle these various elements determines the strength and success of the work that we do.

The emphasis in this series is on practical service founded on basic principles and not on passing fads. Some older ministers need to catch up with the present, while newer ministers need to catch up on the past. We all can learn much from each other if only we're honest enough to admit it and humble enough to accept each other's counsel.

I began pastoring in 1950 and over the years have seen many changes take place in local-church ministry, from bus ministries and house churches to growth groups and megachurches. Some of the changes have been good and are now integrated into God's work in many churches. But some ideas that attracted national attention decades ago now exist only on the pages of forgotten books in used-book stores. How quickly today's exciting headlines become tomorrow's footnotes! "Test everything. Hold on to the good" (1 Thess. 5:21).

An ancient anonymous prayer comes to mind:

From the cowardice that shrinks from new truth,
From the laziness that is content with half-truths,
From the arrogance that thinks it knows all truth,
    O God of truth, deliver us!

Our desire is that both the seasoned servant and the new seminary graduate will find encouragement and enlightenment from the Ministry Dynamics series.

Warren W. Wiersbe

A Brief Theology of Stewardship

Everything belongs to God. That is the perfect place to start whenever we think of money and how we use it in churches. There's not *my* money and *church* money. There's not *program* money and *mission* money, *designated* money and *general-giving* money. No, everything is God's money. Everything. Not 10 percent. Everything.

It's important that we first get the ownership part clear, for as long as we consider only a portion of the resources entrusted to us as God's money, we tend toward error and begin to quibble over minutia. If only part is God's money, then which part? And how big a part? Does the part change from day to day and situation to situation? How much, then, can I claim as my own and not worry about? If I consider it my money to begin with, and I deign to give a certain part of it to God (nice guy that I am), or if I decide to designate part of that money sacred, while the rest remains secular and within my control, then I will come up with a completely different theology of church finance than if I consider it first all God's. If I have ten apples, how many belong to God? Ten, not one.

That's the hard part of a theology of stewardship. It involves a lot more than words and ideas. It involves giving up what, apart from Jesus Christ, I would rightfully claim as my own. In our society very little remains as sacrosanct as money.

I know a pastor who gets a kick out of saying at the annual congregational meeting: "In order to be fair, since at this meeting we will be discussing in public the pastors' salaries, let's just go around the room to start things off, and each of you tell everyone what you make annually. We'll begin with the elders. Bob, what do you make?"

It always elicits a nervous twitter and some awkward moments until people are sure he's only joshing them. Why? Because money is right at the heart of who we are and what we hold as priorities. Money tells all about us, like a child who hasn't yet learned social discretion. We consider financial affairs an extremely private matter. Most people would sooner tell you their sexual sins than their adjusted gross income from last year's 1040.

So a theology that begins with God holding title to all we think *we* possess—that's a difficult starting place. It is, however, the proper place to begin. Anything less denies God's sovereignty and falsely elevates our autonomy.

To Be a Steward

The word *stewardship*, of course, comes from *steward*. Today we lack the model of large estates with stewards looking out for the lord's interests, so maybe we should use the word *guardianship* instead of *steward-*

ship. Since it is a common occurrence for today's sandwich-generation adults to take care of aged parents as their legal guardians, people understand what a *guardian* is. A *steward* or *guardian* does not own the wealth or property; he or she instead simply manages it for the benefit of the legal owner. The wealth or property is placed into the guardian's or steward's care, with the expectation that the steward will not run off with it or convert it to personal use but will instead guard and cultivate the wealth, taking into account the best interests of the proper owner. A steward manages the interests of the owner. *Stewardship*, then, is the activity of taking extremely good care of what belongs to another.

The parable of the talents (Matt. 25:14–30) provides a great case in point. The man in the story entrusted *his* property to his slaves—five talents to one slave, two to another, and one to a third. You know the story: One slave invested the five talents and made another five; the second turned his two talents into four by faithful investment. The one-talent slave merely sat on the one talent given him and, when the master returned, simply gave the talent back to him.

Every one of these three slaves was a steward; each took what belonged to the master, used it, and then returned to the master both the original stake and any investment returns. None of it belonged to the steward. All went back to the master. The designation of "good and trustworthy" went to the two who showed a return on their stewardship, and the scorn of being called "wicked and lazy" fell on the one-talent slave. But in all cases, all the money was the master's money. The slaves were mere stewards, not owners.

Such are we—stewards, not owners. Why? Because of God's sovereignty over creation. "The earth is the

LORD's and all that is in it; the world, and those who live in it," exults David in Psalm 24. The Creator necessarily possesses the creation, just as a playwright or songwriter retains copyright over intellectual property. God made it; it is his.

We are his too. We don't even possess ourselves, as much as postmodern people would like to consider their bodies, their lives, their decisions, their possessions their own. But Paul tells the believers in Corinth: "Do you not know that . . . you are not your own? For you were bought with a price" (1 Cor. 6:19–20). God not only made us in the first place, but he also purchased us at an extraordinary price to be his own possession. We belong not to ourselves but to God.

In that light our possessions surely belong to God. We have what we ostensibly own through gift, inheritance, work, fortuitous experiences. Which of these sources falls outside of God's sovereignty? Could we work, were it not for the strength, intelligence, skills, and even breath that God gives? Can we claim any of the gifts of God's hand as our due? Is anything we call "mine" secured in our possession without God's willing it so? No, apart from the sustaining grace of our Sovereign God, nothing would be ours; nothing would remain ours. All, in truth, is God's.

So that leaves us needing to be stewards of the possessions of the Supreme Other.

To Be a Giver

But why should people give? Why should they transfer from their hands what God has given them? A number of good reasons exist:

- *Giving is good for the giver.* Calvin Miller writes in *The Finale:* "The world is poor because her fortune is buried in the sky and all her treasure maps are of the earth."[1] People's lives will be forever impoverished if they remain ignorant of what is truly valuable. Allowed to hold on to wealth, as if it would satisfy, they will be deceived for life. Simply in letting go, in releasing their grip on their possessions, people gain perspective, if not something more: the joy of giving, dignity, self-respect.

  In *Letters to Scattered Pilgrims,* Gordon Cosby tells of talking with an impoverished widow, years ago, whose four-dollar-a-month offering the deacons felt was too much of a burden for her: "I went and told her of the concern of the deacons. I told her as graciously and as supportively as I knew how that she was relieved of the responsibility of giving. As I talked with her . . . tears came to her eyes. 'I want to tell you,' she said, 'that you are taking away the last thing that gives my life dignity and meaning.'"[2] People need to give.

- *Giving is good for the church.* Other than a few churches with endowments that could keep them going even if no one walked in the door, churches depend on the financial stewardship of their members to underwrite their life and ministries. This obviously has been God's intention from even before the church. Moses delivered the law that "the choicest of the first fruits of your ground you shall bring unto the house of the LORD your God" (Exod. 23:19), and Malachi spoke God's mind: "Bring the full tithe into the storehouse, so that there may be food in my house" (Mal. 3:10). In the early church, Paul urged the new Christians, "On the first day of every week, each of you is to put aside and save whatever extra you earn" for the collection for the church in Jerusalem (1 Cor. 16:2–3). God's method has never been fund-raising through lotteries and sales and car washes; God has always expected the people of faith to support the ministry in and through their community of faith.

- *Giving is good for the recipient of the church's ministry.* The obedient, faithful giving of the saints meets other people's needs. There is much evil to be ameliorated, much hunger to be fed, much suffering to be eased, much ignorance to be erased, much seeking to be met with faith. The gospel must be preached far and wide to all nations. Believers need to be made into disciples. People simply *need* what the church can bring, purchased in part through the material gifts of the people of God. God could rain gold, but God chooses not to so operate. God chooses to bring wholeness through the gifts of his people channeled to the needs of those who will receive the generosity of the church.

- *Giving is good for God.* If our chief end is, as the Westminster Catechism says, "to glorify God and enjoy him forever," then we should give, because giving to God helps to glorify God. Paul told the Ephesians, "In Christ we have also obtained an inheritance, having been destined according to the purpose of him who accomplishes all things according to his counsel and will, so that we, who were the first to set our hope on Christ, might live for the praise of his glory" (Eph. 1:11–12). We do bring praise to God's glory when we give to God from the material blessings he has streamed our way in an inheritance beyond belief. Some religions give out of a sense of fear. Some people heap offerings on altars because of a sense of duty or to curry favor. Christians, however, give in praise to God out of profound thankfulness.

To Be a Corporate Steward

Stewardship, oddly enough, like sin, has both an individual and a corporate side to it. What is true for individuals—that God is the Owner/Landlord—remains even more appropriately true about the church. Not only is the church the Lord's, but its entire reason for being, its "business," is promoting the kingdom of God. While an individual's stewardship is to make appropriate use of God-given time, talent, and treasure, a church's stewardship through its leadership structure is to use appropriately and responsibly the corporate resources entrusted to it by so many individuals.

Church leaders face the tremendous responsibility of being wise stewards of God's gifts placed in their particular body for the purpose of furthering the kingdom of God. While a church leader bears individual responsibility to be a steward personally, he or she also carries an even greater responsibility to manage well the stewardship incumbent on a leader of the church. Such responsibility includes:

- *Teaching and preaching about biblical stewardship.* If the members of the church will be sound stewards, a great responsibility lies on the leaders of the church to make that happen. Stewardship, for most people, arises not from their nature but from a heart turned toward God and God's ways.
- *Setting a fitting example.* A pastor or church leader whose own financial house is out of order will have

a difficult time impressing stewardship on the flock. Likewise, those who give sparingly or grudgingly will generally not produce a generous congregation.

- *Developing and executing wise fiscal plans and sometimes making hard decisions.* Those who misuse or mismanage corporate funds will not be trusted with more, whereas those who manage well (like the good and faithful slave with ten talents) will be given more. For planning, Jesus uses the example of a man who sets out to build a tower but first sits down to estimate the cost to see if he can finish it, or the king who counts his troops before he contemplates going to battle (Luke 14:28–35). So leaders must plan for appropriate and significant uses of the money that is entrusted to the church.

- *Encouraging people to give.* Committed Christians do support the work of the church when they consider the church's plans to be godly and right. It is often amazing what God's people can do with the resources entrusted to them when they understand what God wants them to do. Most often, however, people need encouragement, which Jesus knew well. He had no fear of talking about money.

  According to Howard L. Dayton Jr., writing in *Leadership* journal, "Jesus talked much about money. Sixteen of the thirty-eight parables were concerned with how to handle money and possessions. In the Gospels, an amazing one out of ten verses (288 in all) deals directly with the subject of money. The Bible offers 500 verses on prayer, less than 500 verses on faith, but more than 2,000 verses on money and possessions."[3]

- *Reporting information and accomplishments.* People desire information to make sound personal decisions about financial support of their church, and the leader is the one to supply appropriate and accurate facts. How much money is needed? By when? Why? How will it be used? How does this fit with our ministry plans? These kinds of questions naturally demand thoughtful response. In a like manner, people respond well to reports of what their giving has accomplished. The home built for the Guatemalan peasant family, the staff member hired and the work she is doing, the new overhead projector and how it has helped with praise singing—these publicized products of giving induce repeat giving.

- *Handling money responsibly.* Money is a temptation. Money is a liability. Money is a burden—necessary, but difficult nonetheless. When cash, checks, and gifts come into a church, they must be treated with care. The dependable leader will ease temptation, safeguard funds, and account appropriately for every penny received.

Details of corporate responsibilities such as these fill the remainder of this book. Fred Smith Sr. once wrote, "God entrusts us with money as a test; for, like a toy to the child, it is training for handling things of more value."[4] That we may learn and practice well the greater tasks as we "toy" with money is the purpose of this book.

For Further Reading

Berkley, James D., ed. *Leadership Handbook of Management and Administration.* Grand Rapids: Baker, 1997. The section on finances, beginning on page 403, is comprehensive.

Cunningham, Richard B. *Creative Stewardship*. Nashville: Abingdon, 1979. This volume in Lyle Schaller's Creative Leadership Series explores well the meaning of giving.

McKay, Arthur R. *Servants and Stewards*. Philadelphia: Geneva, 1963. This thin, older book, long out of print, is still worth finding.

Piper, Otto. *The Christian Meaning of Money*. Englewood Cliffs, N.J.: Prentice-Hall, 1965. A fine exposition of the stewardship and ownership of property.

Tennyson, Mack. *Church Finances for People Who Count*. Grand Rapids: Zondervan, 1990. Mack provides a wise layman's approach to the practical aspects of stewardship.

Prudent Practices

In any field of endeavor, some practices simply make more sense than others. In football you don't punt on second down. In driving you don't shift manually without using the clutch. In child raising you don't favor one child over another. Common sense, experience, the realities at hand—all point to practices that reflect generally accepted wisdom.

The same is true in church finance. The wisdom of a number of practices has been proven time and again. Practices such as these *can* be violated. Sometimes a leader or church can do so and escape harm for years. But sooner or later, time and circumstance will catch up with those who break these rules, and harm nearly always results.

The reason we need to follow wise practices is simple and should be known to all Christians: the Fall. Fallen humankind can devise no end of mischief, and these fiscally prudent practices are intended to check the tendency of people toward the misappropriation of both power and common resources.

How *Not* to Do It

I shudder when I recall how a church I once pastored handled money. We were well-intentioned, and I didn't know any better (not a good excuse but a good explanation), but we could have been hurt badly. In that church, when the offering was received, it was brought forward and placed on the communion table during the doxology. So far, so good. After the service, however, our volunteer church treasurer—we'll call her Agnes—would empty the offering into a bank-deposit bag and take it home to count and record. After she had counted the loose change and recorded the amounts from checks and envelopes, she would deposit the money on Monday, or maybe Tuesday if she was busy. Agnes also managed the checking account, wrote and signed checks, and kept all the church books. For large checks, a second signature was needed, but, since it was so inconvenient to find a second signer, Agnes kept a supply of checks already signed by the other person to use when she needed the second signature. All this was a one-woman show, relying completely on the availability, honesty, and accuracy of Agnes.

I have no doubt that Agnes was as honest as the day is long and that she recorded and deposited every penny dropped into our plates. I am convinced emotionally that the checks she wrote were 100 percent legitimate. But how do I *know?* In truth, I don't know. I can only surmise, based on my confidence in Agnes. In reality, Agnes *could* have stuffed her pockets with twenties from the plate. Agnes *could* have endorsed and deposited checks into a phony account under her control. Agnes *could* have written checks from the church account to herself or coconspirators. And we never would have known it.

We who led that church were not following prudent fiscal practices. Had anything gone dreadfully wrong, we could have been held liable as negligent in our responsibilities. Had anything even been alleged, we would have been helpless simply to defend Agnes's integrity, much less to explain the naïveté of our practices. As a young pastor, I sorely needed the counsel of those who understood prudent practices of fiscal responsibility, such as the following.

Set Up a System of Internal Control

The term *internal control* is accounting jargon for a number of practices shrewdly designed to safeguard church income and resources, regulate the disbursement of funds, and protect the integrity and reputation of those charged with handling church money. In the example with Agnes, above, the church and I neglected nearly every element of internal control!

At the heart of internal control is a division of responsibilities. At any point, cash and checks are never left in the possession of only one person. One person is never allowed both to receive and record money, nor can one person both spend and account for the spending. The roles must be split between at least two individuals. This basic reliance on a small team means that for deliberate embezzlement to happen, two or more people must conspire; one person alone cannot work the ill deed when internal control is in place and working. This one element alone can prevent many problems.

Consider the story of Agnes: If internal control had been in operation, Agnes would never have taken the money home. During the service, the money was in the control of at least two ushers or on the communion table in plain sight of everyone. But after Agnes scooped it into a deposit bag, anything could have happened to that money. It could have been stolen from her home. Family members could have removed loose bills. Agnes could have helped herself to the cash.

When money is not to be counted immediately, it should be taken by two unrelated persons for deposit in a bank night depository or locked in a secure church safe. The counting and recording should be done by a team of at least two, who keep a record of the amounts given by each contributor and the total receipts. (If this is a rotating team, no small group of people has knowledge of all the giving patterns, and no group becomes so ensconced that a long-term cover-up is possible.) Then another person should make the actual bank deposit, keeping a receipt. The counters' amount should reconcile with the deposit receipt. Donors should receive a record of their regular giving, at least annually—which Agnes did actually do. Finally, the person keeping the books and making financial reports—Agnes—should not be the same as the one counting or depositing the money.

This separation of responsibilities places a number of checks and balances into effect. The money itself is kept secure: It remains locked in either a bank or safe or in the possession of two or more people; a counter would have to trick or enlist the other counter(s) to take cash; the person making the deposit can't short the amount without it showing up against the counters' record; when donors receive an accounting of their giving and check the amount against their own records, they verify that all their giving is getting to the church; and the ones with access to the cash before it is deposited do not have access to the books to doctor them and cover up embezzlement. This plan provides considerable safety to the money coming in.

Another internal control plan is needed to safeguard the disbursement of money. The key here is for the one who actually writes checks or handles cash to be different from the one who keeps the books—which wasn't the case with Agnes. With this better system, a person can't take money and then cover it up in the books. If the cashier is writing checks to herself or depositing funds in a dummy account, someone else will discover it when doing the bookkeeping. In addition, the one doing the bookkeeping cannot actually get real money into phony accounts without going through another person who disburses the money.

Requiring a second signature on checks above a threshold amount also makes good sense. Two cautious persons must then consider large expenditures before they can be made. One person can never write a large check and run off with it. The two-signature rule, of course, gets absolutely negated when blank checks are signed in advance by the second party "for the sake of convenience." This practice, as was done in my former church for Agnes's sake, should never be allowed.

Abide By the Prudent-Person Rule

No one sets out with the intention of being negligent. It usually just happens because someone doesn't take the extra care *not* to be negligent.

When I had small children and one of them did something like leave a borrowed tool out in the rain, I'd tell them about it. Nearly always the response was something like, "Well, I didn't do it on purpose!" to which I'd reply, "That's true, but you need to be more careful. The saw is just as rusty as it would have been if you *had* left it out on purpose."

According to attorney and CPA Richard Hammar in *Pastor, Church, and Law,* church officers and board members have the legal responsibility to perform their duties "in good faith, in a manner they reasonably believe to be in the best interests of the corporation, and with such care as an ordinary prudent person in a like position would use under similar circumstances."[1] This duty of due care means that church leaders cannot, like my young children, claim immunity from charges of negligence just because their intentions weren't bad. If a normal person using common intelligence and care would be expected to do better, the church leaders can be held to such a standard by the law.

Richard Hammar suggests there is relative safety from charges of negligence when leaders undertake such minimal practices as attending meetings of the board, reviewing financial statements, looking into and correcting any apparent irregularities, operating according to the rules of the organization, going on record in opposition to board actions with which they disagree, and resigning when they can no longer fulfill these responsibilities, because "the law has no place for dummy directors." The church deserves at least a prudent person in a role of responsibility.

Operate under a Sunshine Policy

A sunshine policy encourages complete accountability within the church leadership. Meetings are open. Decisions are fully and accurately recorded and reported to the congregation. Income and expenditures are in the books, and the books are available for inspection. A full disclosure is made of any financial activity to those who need to know. Insider deals are not allowed; interested parties abstain from decision making. Financial mistakes or embarrassments are not kept from the congregation. In short, there are no deals and no secrets with a sunshine policy.

Most civil governments operate with sunshine rules, and denominational bodies often have adopted such a policy. Yes, the doors can be closed briefly for specific business, such as negotiations for the purchase of property or for sensitive personnel matters. Yes, in most churches, the amounts individuals give are kept confidential, and many churches choose to keep specific salary figures on a need-to-know basis. But in general, with a sunshine policy, the doors are flung wide open.

This liberal policy makes it harder for anything underhanded or self-serving to happen within church business. When secrets are kept, when sweetheart deals are made and hidden, when errors are buried, when a small, powerful coterie rules and no one else is privy to the deliberations—trouble comes quickly. A sunshine policy serves the dual purpose of making evil more difficult while involving the congregation in its own governance.

Follow the Church's Bylaws and Constitution Exactly

The express line to buy trouble runs directly *around* the church's polity. When bylaws and a constitution have been adopted, a leader *must* follow them or be liable for significant consequences. If there are *no* rules, a leader fares better than if there are rules that aren't followed.

That means we are wise to become well acquainted with church organizational documents. Who is able to sign the note if the church borrows money? What body approves or modifies the church budget? Can the church loan money to a pastor for a down payment on a house—and at what rate? How is a Finance Committee member replaced midterm? For questions such as these, the church constitution and bylaws need to be consulted. If these documents provide a method that the leaders fail to use, the leaders may be held personally liable for their actions in a court of law!

Uphold Fiduciary Responsibilities

Churches, as the body of Christ, are meant to glorify God and serve others. Churches, as nonprofit corporations, are meant to benefit the general public. Thus church *leaders* are meant to function in such a way that the *organization* benefits, not the individual leaders themselves. They are to act in the organization's best interests, not their own.

Certainly pastors, of all people, ought to be prepared to work in a way to benefit the flock rather than fatten the shepherd. If Jesus had harsh words for the hireling who merely neglected the sheep, what would he have to say about a mutton fiend who systematically devours the flock?

In a similar way, the government takes no liking to the person who neglects fiduciary responsibility in order to arrange personal gain from an organization given tax-exempt status to benefit society as a whole. No individual is meant to profit from a tax-exempt corporation, no pastor or lay leader from a church. That means such activities as sweetheart loans to insiders (including pastors), insider deals to relatives or principals, contracts given to friends or associates over lower bidders, or anything motivated by self-interest must be avoided.

Honor Fund Designations and Donor Intent

It is not unusual for even the smallest churches to have a number of funds—general fund, missions fund, building fund, youth camp fund, memorial fund, and so on—and for large churches to have dozens. Often the actual money from several funds gets thrown into one bank account, although accounting keeps separate records of the fund amounts. All is well until unaccounted money starts flowing between funds.

This usually happens innocently enough. It's August and the general fund is empty but the memorial fund has several thousand dollars in the Mayberry Memorial Account waiting for the bell tower to be built. Payroll needs to be met. So the church treasurer asks if she can transfer a few thousand from the Mayberry money into the general fund "until things pick up in the fall." It makes sense, to avoid borrowing or not meeting payroll, but then the furnace goes out in the fall, and everybody forgets to transfer the money back into the Mayberry account. Church books easily get messed up in this manner.

The problem is, it's not only bad policy but also illegal. Money given for a designated purpose cannot be diverted permanently to undesignated causes. The church basically has an agreement with the donor, and when the money is used in ways other than those agreed on, the church is at fault. An audit will discover when designated money from a restricted fund gets used for general purposes in the operating fund.

The best way to avoid this problem is to keep funds separate, or at least to build a high wall between restricted funds and unrestricted funds. When the summer pinch comes and the church needs to borrow internally, it is best to transfer other nonrestricted funds into the operating fund—with a mechanism and reminder to return the borrowed money to the correct fund before the end of the fiscal year.

Funds restricted by donor intention should not be redirected to other uses, such as the operating fund. If, for whatever reasons, such funds do get temporarily diverted to another use, they *must* be replaced in short order so that the fund remains intact when it is needed for its designated purpose.

At times donor stipulations can become tremendously onerous for the receiving institution. For instance, a congregation may intend to build a modern building, but a donor may give many thousands of dollars to be used only for a Gothic-style bell tower. A church then has to decide if it can with integrity accept the gift. The church can turn down the gift or seek to have the terms broadened. What the church cannot do is accept the gift and then use it in ways contrary to the stipulated purpose, however outrageous those stipulations may appear.

Gifts given with stipulations by donors who are unable to be contacted, are deceased, or are presently unknown *may* be redirected through a legal process. At least thirty-one states have adopted a version of the Uniform Management of Institutional Funds Act. This act allows a governing board to petition a specific civil court for release of the restriction imposed on the gift. Generally the courts try to stay as close as possible to the original intent, while allowing the church to avoid cases where it is impossible or impractical to honor the restrictions.

Practice Fiscally Conservative, Nonspeculative Investment Management

Church funds are not the stake to use to make a killing on Wall Street. When a church is holding cash for a time, it is prudent to invest it in a way that provides a return. Burying it in coffee cans in the church yard would not be prudent, nor would keeping it absolutely safe in a noninterest-bearing checking account during even moderately inflationary times. But the question arises: What financial instruments should be used? bonds? stocks? mutual funds? money-market accounts? certificates of deposit? church investment funds or denominational programs?

It is impossible to give that kind of advice quickly, universally, and safely. The general rule of thumb, however, is fiscal conservatism. Preservation of assets takes precedence over growth or speculation. Many churches operate under the policy that donated stock gets sold immediately, to prevent the temptation to speculate and possibly lose value. Get-rich-quick schemes should be out of the question, especially those that involve a parishioner or the relative of one. Such speculative investments as commodities, derivatives, penny stocks, junk bonds, and Brother Lester's can't-lose new restaurant enterprise should never be considered by churches.

Recently even well-established, respected parachurch organizations, church colleges, and some denominations faced multimillion-dollar losses from a clever double-your-money offer that turned into a pyramid scheme. While no church wants to believe that a swindler would target the house of God, history, sadly, tells us otherwise. The old adage is true for churches as well as for individuals: If it seems too good to be true, it probably is.

Make Certain the Church Is Incorporated

The old public service announcement asked: "It's ten o'clock. Do you know where your children are?" A public service announcement for churches might read: "At this moment do you know if your congregation is incorporated?"

When a local church is incorporated as a nonprofit corporation, the congregation itself is an entity. If something awful happens, the corporation gets sued. If money is owed, the corporation owes it. In some states, an incorporated church doesn't have to pay property taxes.

But if the congregation was never incorporated, or if the incorporation has lapsed due to a failure to keep it current, the church is no longer considered a legal entity in itself. That means the *individuals* can sometimes be sued if someone breaks a leg in the parking lot, or the individuals can possibly be held liable to pay debts. (The individuals held accountable are likely to be officers or other leaders or those with the deepest pockets.) A lack of nonprofit incorporation may mean in some states that the church has to pay taxes like any other organization or individual.

Richard Hammar, generally recognized as the expert in such matters, advises in *Pastor, Church, and Law:*

> The legal disabilities connected with the unincorporated association form of organization causes many churches to incorporate. . . . the members of a church corporation ordinarily are shielded from personal liability for the debts and misconduct of other members or agents of the church, and for the obligations of the church staff.[2]

The prudent procedure is to be certain of your church's status. Ordinarily this can be found by checking with the state secretary of state's office. Most pastors assume their church is incorporated. That can be a shocking assumption to have proven incorrect.

Provide Proper Insurance and Bonding

At the least, faithful church leaders will make sure the church carries adequate insurance for its facilities and for liability. Risk management has become complicated, and people differ over the amount of insurance to provide, the risks to be covered by insurance versus those to be assumed by the church, the types of hazard to insure against, and even what agent offers the best deal. Aside from these debates, however, the need remains: adequate, appropriate, current insurance is a necessity for any church.

Congregations in which bookkeepers, financial secretaries, and volunteer counters, clerks, and treasurers will be handling large amounts of money need to consider the advisability of having key persons bonded. This can provide protection for the congregation and peace of mind for all.

Everyone knows Murphy's Law: If something can go wrong, it will. In the world of church finance, we know another law as well: "All have sinned and fall short of the glory of God" (Rom. 3:23). With our eyes wide open to what *may* go wrong, we seek protection by following these few prudent practices.

For Further Reading

Busby, Daniel. *The Zondervan Church and Nonprofit Organization Tax and Financial Guide.* Grand Rapids: Zondervan, 2000. Published yearly, this guide offers tips, examples, and current information.

Chaffee, Paul. *Accountable Leadership: Resources for Worshipping Communities.* San Francisco: ChurchCare Publishing, 1993. A remarkably thorough guide to moral and responsible leadership behavior.

Hammar, Richard. *Pastor, Church, and Law.* 2d ed. Matthews, N.C.: Christian Ministry Resources, 1991. This book is the bible of church tax and legal references.

Planning and Budgeting

Anything worth doing is worth planning to do well. In particular, something as vital as a church's financial foundation demands careful thought and planning. The alternative to church planning and budgeting is indiscriminate spending, flying blind, knowing neither where you're going nor how you expect to get there.

A budget serves as a statement of purpose. It announces to the world the church's priorities. It shows the congregation where their efforts are headed. It guides the pastor and leaders in their policy decisions. A budget channels the resources of the church into the work of the church in a thoughtful, purposeful way, unique to that congregation. Prepared well and used appropriately, a budget provides order and direction to the activities of a congregation.

Prepared thoughtlessly and used slavishly, a budget can be a moronic master, mindlessly hindering ministry, squelching spontaneity, and engulfing leaders in dreary busywork. A budget should never displace the Holy Spirit: "Sorry, can't witness to that poor soul. There's nothing in the budget for it." A budget that remains suspiciously like that of the previous year will most likely drag down a ministry into a static status quo. Instead, a proper church budget ought to stretch imaginations, cause a slight gasp, expand vision, and enable ministry.

So just what is the process that produces the ministry-enhancing servant rather than an action-stultifying master? It begins with a serious examination of values and priorities.

Fund-raising Philosophies

Churches vary in their approach to stewardship and fund-raising, and one of the highest divides is the question of a unified budget versus a series of special appeals. Do you put all your begs in one ask-it? Or do you highlight needs as they come along and invite people to support them? If these methods represent the two poles, a given church's philosophy usually will fall somewhere in the spectrum between.

Some churches operate under the assumption that people carefully plan their giving and don't appreciate being continually harangued for more money. Churches with this philosophy make a budget, ask for pledges once a year, and basically stay out of the asking business the rest of the year. When a special need or emergency arises, this kind of church finds funds within the budget and does not approach the congregation for "extra mile" giving.

There is much to recommend this system. When both the leadership and the congregation consider their stewardship responsibilities seriously, even sacrificially, this system has great integrity. If the leadership prayerfully seeks God's counsel and sets a budget goal worthy of what God intends to do through that congregation and if the individual members search their souls and open their hearts and pocketbooks to be faithful to God in their giving, the resultant budget and pledge underwriting represent a significant statement of dedication to God.

Nobody is playing games. The church isn't playing bait and switch: "All you need to do is pledge (but we'll also be asking you repeatedly for more money because we didn't plan well or we think you're holding back)." The members don't have to artfully lower their pledged amount to hold back a reserve because they know they'll look bad if they have nothing to give at the inevitable series of special appeals. No, both church and member can pray and plan and pledge and pay in a decent, orderly, systematic, expected way.

The system has drawbacks, however. It is so very cut-and-dried that it lacks the emotion and spontaneity that enlivens much Christian giving. Events arise that genuinely inspire giving, but if the church is locked into a rigid one-ask system, the moment is lost. Needs cannot always be anticipated—a flood, the church burns down, refugees stream into town—and an inflexible budget may well be unable to handle the strain. In addition, people in the church constantly are being inundated with appeals from colleges, relief agencies, and other causes. If the church asks only once a year, and yet people are making giving decisions multiple times a year, the church may lose ground in the giving process.

For these reasons and others, some churches operate in a similar manner but make a number of planned exceptions throughout the year for special offerings that people generally know are coming, say, a Christmas offering, One Great Hour of Sharing, a missions offering, a youth fund-raiser, and sometimes even a rare special appeal in an emergency. These churches restrict the number of special appeals, feeling they have a contract of sorts with the congregation that they won't pester them with countless appeals, once they've prayerfully determined their giving and settled into their pledged amount through systematic giving. But churches in this group do use a special appeal several times a year.

Flexibility is one of the advantages of this system. The church makes an honest attempt to anticipate needs and write them into the budget, but it also has the flexibility to meet unexpected or increased needs through a special offering. The people, when they pledge, have the reasonable assurance that they won't be asked often to give above the pledged amount. They can stretch themselves with the pledge and still maintain a little reserve for over-and-above giving they anticipate throughout the year. The truth is that most pledgers and even tithers *do* have the ability and even desire to give beyond their pledged amounts as God moves their hearts. This system allows for that added devotion. It has the benefit of being organized and somewhat predictable, while also allowing the Spirit to move in new ways.

The only negative factor is the hybrid nature of this middle way. It is neither fully planned nor broadly spontaneous, and so it loses the pure advantage of either system. Although people plan and pledge, they can still be surprised with a special appeal. But, on the other side, there are probably a lot of needs that never merit a special offering in this system. If the church conscientiously limits the special appeals, many needs will not make it to the importance threshold that warrants an offering.

Churches like these can expect a running debate over how many special offerings are too many or what kinds of fund-raising activities are allowed. For this reason, a church fund-raising policy statement often proves invaluable. Such a statement outlines the church's philosophy about fund-raising, provides examples of approved and disapproved kinds of activities (bingo? lotteries? sales of items? on Sundays? who keeps the profits? special offerings? fees for attendance?), and offers guidelines for the approval and operation of such activities. Wrestling through these questions once for overall policy approval means that they won't need to be argued every time a request arises.

A third general philosophy of giving does away with the unified budget and pledges and simply operates with more spontaneity and emotion. When the leaders sense God's call, they move ahead, inviting the people to join them. They know God isn't lacking in resources and won't take them where he won't supply their needs, and so when a need arises, they go to God's people to meet that need. A new roof, a missions initiative, a speaker coming through town, meeting payroll—all these items are laid before the people and an offering is taken. The church moves as God leads; the people give as the needs are expressed and God stirs them.

This model can be highly spontaneous and immediately faithful. When a Paul comes through town for a collection for Jerusalem, this group doesn't have to find a budget line item to draw from or decide if this qualifies as one of the few yearly appeals. The saints can see and respond to the many needs of the church, not being insulated from them through budgets and boards. Members learn discernment and mercy, being given a wealth of opportunities to give. And God may just surprise planner-types who can't comprehend the church operating responsibly with such a spontaneous method. When the people come through to meet even seemingly overwhelming needs, God is glorified.

On the down side, this system can lead to financial chaos and perpetual arm-twisting. Some organizations using this system become like a disaster-of-the-week club, wherein every service requires an extended appeal to "just keep the lights on" or "help the blind baby orphans." Givers become jaded to appeals, which then need to be cranked up a notch or two emotionally. It is hard for the church to plan income and expenses responsibly when they vary tremendously with appeals, and keeping track of special giving designated to a specific cause becomes an accounting nightmare. More routine needs that must be met (such as rewiring the building, buying copy paper) get pushed aside for the more glamorous causes that people like to support (such as mission causes, winsome personalities, bricks and mortar).

The remainder of this chapter deals more with the first two models, since the third model is, by nature, more spontaneous and unplanned. If a church decides that a little more spiritual planning is in order, here is a direction to head.

Deciding Church Priorities

A budget says what's important to a church and how it will be supported. Thus the first step in planning and budgeting is for a church to decide what it considers important. What will be the church priorities? If only some things out of a vast spectrum of activities can be accomplished, what should they be? What do we hold dear?

Too often churches plow ahead without going through this process. If there was a budget the previous year, it gets tinkered with a little for inflation and program changes and is sent on down as the next year's budget. But this leads to institutional drift. Perhaps at one time one group of leaders considered various items of such significance that they put them into the budget for a specified amount, but is that still the desire of this group of leaders at this time? If a budget is truly to represent the will of the church for the mission of the church, this early business of prioritizing must be worked through.

A clean sheet of paper is a great place to start. A single question can focus the thinking: If we were to support nothing else as a congregation, what ten (or twenty or whatever) items would we be sure to fund? Answers will probably be ventured, such as keep the building available, useable, and safe; support the Rileys in New Guinea; keep our pastor and staff paid and supported; pass on the faith to the children and youth. Pull out as many answers as possible.

The next step is to prioritize the answers. Critical thinking is needed here. Are they all equally important? Which are essential? What is most important? How do the items fit into a ranking? This exercise obviously will produce a number of opinions that differ and often conflict. The key is to work toward a consensus by asking the questions of comparison: If you simply had to choose between *a* and *b*, and you couldn't have both, which would you choose?

At the end of this rigorous process, there ought to be a list of church priorities that are ranked from top to bottom. These items the church considers of key importance. It is these items that the church feels it *must* budget for. Below these items will probably be some disputable items from special interests, such as add dual-pane windows to the fellowship hall or purchase a riding mower. Again, these ought to be ranked from most important to most expendable. Some of these will probably make it into the budget; others won't. Below these swing items and preferably off the list are the items with practically no support or justifiable purpose, such as hula hoops for the seniors group or a Miata for the associate pastor.

This planning time is important. It may require a series of meetings or at least one long session. It won't be easy, but it establishes what this body at this time considers worth doing and funding, and that's at the heart of what a budget is intended to do.

Building a Chart of Accounts

Given the church's priorities, the next step is to place those items into a budget. Most often this is done by building a chart of accounts, the set of line items that become the separate accounts within a budget. Since most bookkeeping and budgeting is done by computer now, each line item needs not only a name but also an account number. If a church plans to pay the pastor, it will need a line item and account number for "pastor's salary." Other line items for "housing allowance," "auto allowance," "medical and pension," and so on probably need to be included as well. If the church pays for a building, line items for "mortgage," "insurance," "utilities," "maintenance," and so on are called for. In this manner, each of the priorities gets placed onto the chart of accounts.

Exactly how intricate to make the chart of accounts is a judgment call. For utilities, as an example, should there be separate line items for electricity, gas, water, garbage, and sewer, or should they be lumped together under "utilities"? It depends on how closely the financial wizards want to track expenses. The more intricate the chart of accounts, the more numbers need to be posted and, therefore, the more precise information the budget delivers. Ultimately those who want and use the figures need to decide if the added line items are useful or just clutter the report.

And the phone bill—should it be lumped with "utilities" or "office expenses"? Again, those kinds of calls need to be made by those needing the information a budget and financial report generate. There is no right or wrong answer for a question like this. The matter is determined more by the categories of "useful" or "unhelpful."

Most churches do deem it useful to block similar expenses together into sections of the chart of accounts. Thus the budget ends up with chunks of line items in larger sections, such as "personnel," "office," "buildings and grounds," "worship and music," "children and youth," "missions," and so on. Such categories make it easier to find specific line items, and their subtotals give an idea of how large a portion of the budget is being given to various realms of church life.

With a chart of accounts, persons authorizing various expenditures will know which line item to charge. As they look at the budget and financial reports, they will know how much the church has allotted for that kind of expense and they'll know how much has been spent and how much remains.

An annotated chart of accounts contains an explanation for each of the line items. This can be most useful after the architects of the budget rotate out of the picture. For instance, a line item in the personnel budget for "outside events" may mean that it is money to allow employees to attend outside events that charge a fee, or it may be for paying the janitor's overtime when outside groups use the building. Unless the one who created the line item is still around, current leaders may not know. An annotated chart of accounts, however, dispels confusion over the intended use of any particular line item. It also helps the treasurer or program leaders charge expenses to the appropriate account.

Figuring the Expenses

The chart of accounts provides the skeleton of the budget, but no figures are yet attached to the items. Thus the next step is to provide the best guesses of what the various items will cost. A computer spreadsheet, such as Microsoft Excel, proves an efficient way to manage the budget numbers. Once it is set up properly, a spreadsheet makes automatic adjustments to subtotals and totals when a line item is changed.

At this point, it's best to ignore totals. The task at hand is to produce the most accurate forecasts of the annual cost of the ministry priorities reflected in the chart of accounts. This task is full of facts to run down and decisions to make: How much to pay the pastor? What's the percentage that goes into her pension plan? How much do you think electricity prices will go up this year?

The fact-finding probably is best done by an individual or small team, but the policy decisions need to be made by the leadership. In most churches, various units propose their budget requests: The Youth Department asks for program money and an intern; the Choir needs to buy more music and some risers; Missions is asking for a greater percentage of overall giving.

Here's where the already-established priorities come into play. It's possible for a church simply to add up every request without discernment to get a total—which is usually outrageous. This method leads quickly to a form of gamesmanship, where departments ask for much more than they expect to receive and then have room to fall back to a more reasonable figure when reality sets in.

A better method is to bring together all the interested parties and let them hear and question the requests of each group. Thus the church leadership is able both to see the broad picture and to begin to understand how the priorities previously set impinge on the raw requests. Impossible, budget-breaking requests are harder to float when all of the other ministry areas have their own obvious, legitimate needs for a part of the budget pie.

One church does this on a fall Saturday morning. Each ministry area is allotted five to ten minutes to present, explain, justify, and sometimes even defend their written budget request for the next year. The 150-minute meeting proves to be one of the most productive of the year in helping all the leaders understand the scope of the ministries and possibilities in every corner of church life. It also helps them become less defensive of their own budget turf and see the bigger picture.

Projecting Income

When the leadership has decided on the appropriate figure for each line item in the chart of accounts, the expense portion of the proposed budget is complete. Then comes the reality check as the income portion takes shape. The chart of accounts should have entries for income sources as well as expenses. Most churches receive the bulk of their income through the Sunday offering, but even that amount can be divided into sources such as pledged income (often in numbered envelopes), loose-plate income (the untraceable bills and change dropped in the plate), and contributions (unpledged checks and cash in envelopes). Other income sources include such things as special gifts and bequests, rent, income from sales, and interest.

Any church with a history and financial records can make a good estimate for many of these income sources. If the church has a pledge drive, the amount of pledged income is reasonably assured. Historical patterns for loose-plate offering and contributions help leaders estimate for the following year. And they should be able to plan on other sources, such as rent or interest, with some accuracy. Most churches tend to err slightly on the conservative side in income estimation, in order not to spend at a rate that cannot be sustained. While church leaders want to include faith in their projections, if God has been blessing the church in a certain pattern for years, good justification needs to be made for claims that the blessings will flow at a much faster rate the following year.

Once figures are in place for each income source, the total gives the expected extent of the income pool from which to accomplish what the expense side of the budget calls priorities. Rare is the church with more income than projected expenses! If that is your case, praise God and prepare to give more to missions. More often than not, however, the opposite is true: Dreams and vision often exceed dollars and cents.

Balancing Expenses and Income

Unless a church has (1) a "sugar daddy" who will step in to make up any deficit, (2) a significant carryover of funds from previous years to serve as a cushion, or (3) an endowment that will subsidize operating expenses—not a good idea, by the way, in most circumstances, as nice as it sounds (see chapter 7)—the expense side and the income side of the budget must be brought into balance. Other than the ways noted above, there are two main means for creating the balance: decreasing expenses or increasing income.

Decreasing Expenses

You thought each expense was a priority or you would not have included it in the budget. But if there is no income to pay for a portion of the expenses, God must have a different idea. It is time to lower the sights a little. Again there are two choices: an across-the-board decrease or selective cuts.

The across-the-board belt-tightening appears to be a fair method. If there is pain to be had, everyone gets a similar ache. Share and share alike. In most churches, however, this doesn't work well. First, some line items are fixed expenses that cannot bear a decrease, such as loan repayments, some utilities, and commitments to a denomination. A decrease in other line items may cause undue distress, such as cutting long-standing commitments to missionaries, letting staff go, or ending a valuable program.

In addition, uniform cuts may diminish the very programs that help *produce* income or church vitality. For instance, a 10 percent cut in a tremendously effective but financially struggling nursery program may kill the church's best draw for visitors. In general a uniform decrease in every line item proves to be a mind-less and ineffective way to balance the budget.

The other way to decrease expenses is to reenter the negotiation process about the church's true *priorities*. Just as everyone can't be special without losing the meaning of *special*, so *every* item in a church's budget can't be a priority. This is the time for sharp pencils; critical, evaluative thinking; and interdepartmental statesmanship. Something—perhaps a number of things—must be cut, so what is it the church simply *must* do compared to what it would very much *like* to do? A combination of selective cutbacks, some eliminations, and a measure of general conservation in spending usually can be worked out, allowing the congregation to accomplish its mission while matching its expected expenses with its forecasted income.

Increasing Income

But a much happier solution to an out-of-balance budget is to increase income. Had many of the great figures in world missions or church revival looked only at the expense side of the equation, they never would have accomplished what they did. Instead of lowering expenses, they found new income. Two general routes are open to increased income: new sources or greater income from current sources.

New sources may be a surprise. A Presbyterian church camp was experiencing a severe income shortage. Years before, each of the churches in the presbytery was encouraged to give a dollar a member a year to the camp, but interest and even knowledge of the giving program had waned. With an act as simple as adding the line "A buck for Buck Creek Camp" to the presbytery pledge forms sent to each congregation, the camp began to receive many thousands of extra dollars a year from an income source that hadn't been cultivated for years. In a similar way, churches may overlook income sources, such as renting unused space to nonprofit organizations or benevolence from sister churches.

Probably even more promising for increased income, however, is greater giving by current sources. If every party currently giving to a typical church would tithe, most churches would have at least three to four times their current income! The increased capacity to give is present in most current givers. Other current sources of income may be able to yield further increases, such as higher rents, freewill offerings at currently free events, and higher event charges for such activities as camps or youth activities.

It is a balancing act every time a budget is forged. Hard decisions rear their heads. Nothing is easy. But the process helps the church leaders examine what is truly important, truly necessary, truly at the heart of ministry. And God has a marvelous way of providing exactly what is necessary to do the ministry he calls the church to perform.

Examining Cash Flow

There's one more facet of the budget to examine before we can rest easy: the *cash flow*. Cash flow describes the rate at which money arrives at the church through income and departs through expenses. It is altogether possible that a given church in a given year can take in $100,000, spend $95,000, and yet endure the entire year feeling broke. The problem? Cash flow. Expenses came at an earlier part of the year than income.

Figure 1

Cash Flow, St. Marks-on-the-Grid Church

	Jan	Feb	Mar	April	May
Monthly Income	$ 8,000	$ 8,000	$ 8,000	$ 8,000	$ 8,000
Cumulative Income	$ 8,000	$ 16,000	$ 24,000	$ 32,000	$ 40,000
Monthly Expenses	$ 10,000	$ 7,000	$ 7,000	$ 7,000	$ 7,000
Cumulative Expenses	$ 10,000	$ 17,000	$ 24,000	$ 31,000	$ 38,000
Net Income	-$ 2,000	-$ 1,000	$ 0	$ 1,000	$ 2,000

Consider this church's cash flow (see chart). For the months of January through May, the church took in $8,000 a month. Then in the doldrums of summer, the monthly income fell to $6,000 a month. September picked up, and through November the church again received $8,000 a month. Then in December, people caught up with their pledges and felt generous, giving the church $18,000, much of it around Christmas. This "hockey stick effect" (see figure 2 on page 52) is extremely common in churches, with the income line remaining rather flat through most of the year and then shooting up dramatically at the end.

Church spending took a different turn. A big event in January pushed that month's spending to $10,000. Then February through June, spending leveled out at $7,000 a month. Summer activities made July and August cost $8,500 apiece, September's Sunday school kickoff made that a $9,000 month, and then October and November were $7,000 months. In December last-chance budget spending made the expenses $10,000.

At that rate, throughout January and February, the church was as much as $2,000 in the hole. March through June the church was breaking even or ahead. In the period of July through November, however, the church was always behind, as much as $5,000 in Sep-

Figure 1 *(continued)*
Cash Flow, St. Marks-on-the-Grid Church

June	July	Aug	Sept	Oct	Nov	Dec
$ 6,000	$ 6,000	$ 6,000	$ 8,000	$ 8,000	$ 8,000	$ 18,000
$ 46,000	$ 52,000	$ 58,000	$ 66,000	$ 74,000	$ 82,000	$100,000
$ 7,000	$ 8,500	$ 8,500	$ 9,000	$ 7,000	$ 7,000	$ 10,000
$ 45,000	$ 53,500	$ 62,000	$ 71,000	$ 78,000	$ 85,000	$ 95,000
$ 1,000	-$ 1,500	-$ 4,000	-$ 5,000	-$ 4,000	-$ 3,000	$ 5,000

tember. Finally in the last week of December the church climbed out of negative numbers and actually ended the year $5,000 in the black. For seven months of the year, finances looked bleak, even though it was a good year. Cash flow tells an interesting story.

Good church financial planners will forecast and chart cash flow to anticipate and prepare for problem months—typically summer and early fall. The best way to forecast cash flow is to spread each income and expense line item into twelve monthly segments. Some line items will be spent all at once while others are regular monthly expenses. For instance, if a line item is for a youth backpacking trip, it can be forecast to be spent entirely, say, in July. A personnel item probably will be divided somewhat evenly throughout the months since the rate of pay remains constant. History from the last couple of years helps a treasurer forecast both income and expenses month by month.

Once the income and expenses are assigned to the months they will come in or be spent, a simple chart like the one above can be turned into a graph, which shows cumulative income with one line and cumulative expenses with another (see figure 3 on page 53). When the income line stays above the expense line, the church is in the black. When it falls below the

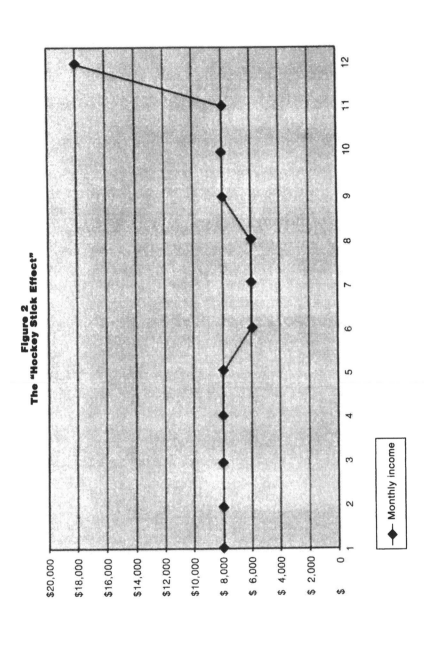

Figure 2
The "Hockey Stick Effect"

Monthly income

Figure 3
Cash Flow, St. Marks-on-the-Grid Church

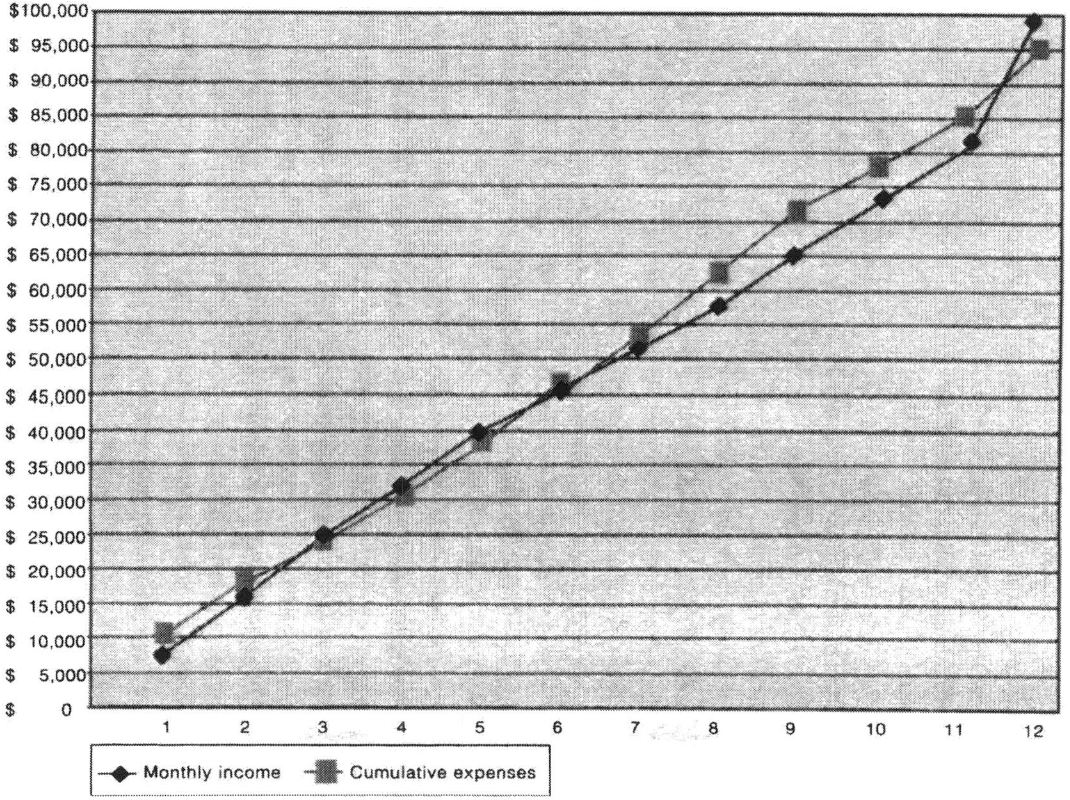

Legend:
- ◆ Monthly income
- ■ Cumulative expenses

expense line, the church is in a deficit situation. The measure of the greatest negative disparity between the two lines marks the amount of reserve (or borrowing ability) the church must have to make it through the year. In the example graph, the church would need to enter the year with at least $5,000 in reserve to make it through September.

With cash flow forecasting, a church is not surprised when August rolls around and making payroll is difficult. At the beginning of the year plans can be made to (1) delay discretionary spending, (2) bring a cash cushion into the year, and/or (3) borrow short-term to cover the cash flow deficiency. Planning and budgeting, after all, are intended to give the church the resources it needs to perform the ministry it is called to do.

For Further Reading

Berkley, James D., ed. *Leadership Handbook of Management and Administration.* Grand Rapids: Baker, 1997. Articles on budgeting and cash flow.

Pollock, David R. *Business Management in the Local Church.* Chicago: Moody, 1996. Pollock goes into beginning and advanced budgeting.

Tennyson, Mack. *Church Finances for People Who Count.* Grand Rapids: Zondervan, 1990. This professor of accountancy has a great section on various budgeting methods.

Raising Money

Most pastors don't enter the ministry for the delightful opportunity to raise money—or really to think about it much, for that matter. Pastors want to preach and teach and counsel and pray. Conducting the annual stewardship campaign ranks way down on the list for most pastors, somewhere near cleaning up after junior high banana night and handling irate phone calls.

Yet the financial strength of a congregation determines much about its spiritual life and effectiveness. And, like it or not, the pastor plays a leading role in the general financial tenor of the congregation. Rare is the thriving congregation whose pastor remains distant from all things financial.

Attitude means a lot. Will money be a taboo subject in church life, a sadly necessary evil at best, an embarrassing topic better left untouched but periodically hauled out because of dire need and then dealt with perfunctorily? Or, on the other extreme, will talk of dollars and giving seemingly intrude into every facet of church life, coloring evangelism with the need for a greater number of givers, turning every sermon into a plea for money, converting church life into a circus of commerce? Or will sound financial policies and a healthy, unabashed enthusiasm for stewardship undergird and strengthen all of church life?

Attitudes are highly contagious, and the pastor's attitude about money washes across a congregation. Over time, a stingy, scared, hoarding pastor will typically produce an overly cautious, tightfisted, selfish congregation, afraid or unwilling to venture. An embarrassed, apologetic pastor, highly reticent when it comes to the topic of money, will usually teach a church to consider money a forbidden topic, a subject highly personal, even distasteful, and not to be brought up in nice company. A boisterous, huckstering, scheming, fly-by-night pastor, who is *always* producing a flashy new way to harvest more money, will sow attitudes in the congregation of irresponsibility, materialism, exploitation, greed, and often simple avoidance.

But the pastor who evokes a quiet sense of credibility, who treats stewardship as an important but not supreme factor of Christian discipleship, who radiates the expectation of God's ability to provide, who inspires confidence by fiscal knowledge and personal commitment, who demonstrates personally the meaning of sacrificial giving, who can speak unabashedly, without hype about giving, who loves God and doesn't want to see God's work hindered by meager giving—this kind of pastor will be effective as a spiritual leader encouraging proper stewardship.

The Pastor's Roles

A pastor plays a number of roles in the stewardship life of a congregation, such as:

- *Resident fiscal theologian.* People understand supporting an organization. They already support Little League and the Opera Guild, activities that require generous participants or benefactors to help foot the bill. What many people *don't* understand is stewardship—God's ownership of our lives and possessions and our need to return a significant portion to God's work. Every church needs a resident fiscal theologian to explain how a church, calling for life commitment from its people, is different from Little League, which needs supporters.
- *Knowledgeable leader.* The maxim states that "knowledge is power," and that is true in the church as well. People want to follow someone who understands the big picture in church finances. Various people may know their individual fiefdoms within the church, but someone needs to be able to guide and interpret the entire ministry. Ignorance of the church's finances hinders a leader's authority and effectiveness.

  But understanding where the church is and where it might be able to go, how it is doing, where the pinch points are, and what to do about them— this kind of information is needed by an effective pastor and useful for furthering the ministry. In addition, when the pastor demonstrates knowledge and ability with finances, the people can rest assured that their church is in able hands and money is not being wasted.
- *Ethicist and arbiter.* In any church, disputes will arise about the apportioning or uses of church money. While sound church policies will handle some problems, others need personal attention. "Is it right to spend church money to buy Cokes for our teens?" "Hey! I don't think the choir is getting its

fair share of the budget." "Doesn't that stewardship slogan seem awfully full of self-interest?"
Someone needs to help church members sort out
right and wrong, fair and unfair.

- *Visionary and cheerleader.* Organizations easily get
  stuck in neutral and need someone to shift them
  into gear. A key pastoral-leadership role is to set
  the vision and cheer people toward it. The good
  pastor uses gentle nudges, stirring assurances, and
  faithful expositions of Scripture to lift the congregation toward heightened financial discipleship. At times the pastor must take on the role of
  champion for bold new thrusts. A stewardship program, a special offering, or a capital campaign will
  likely limp along without the pastor's genuine
  endorsement and enthusiastic support.

- *Trusted source of information.* Sometimes the pastor
  is the source of stewardship information, such as
  in stewardship sermons, pastoral letters in the
  church newsletter, explanations of new initiatives,
  announcements, public forums, and personal
  consultations. Other times the pastor is able to
  point to the one who has the information—the
  church bookkeeper, the campaign chairperson,
  the Finance Committee elder, the Building Committee treasurer. At all times a pastor needs to be
  able to provide trusted, reliable, accurate information about the finances to maintain the people's confidence and goodwill.

A pastor, while key, cannot be the only person involved in a stewardship campaign. In truth, a team of
leaders needs to work through a process that produces
stewardship knowledge, assent, and commitment in
members of the congregation—and raises money.

The Stewardship Campaign

While there exists a number of detailed techniques for annual stewardship campaigns—each with its champions who will swear theirs is the *only* way to do it effectively—a few principles run throughout all of the techniques, namely: (1) forge a compelling vision, (2) introduce a concrete plan, and (3) produce clear communication.

A Compelling Vision

People don't get excited and rally around the mundane. They do, however, flock to persons and ideas that are compelling, bold, and full of vision. They will dust off their checkbooks to support what stirs and inspires them.

A certain way to stunt stewardship is to say to the congregation, in effect, "Well, we're not really sure where we're going as a church, so we just kind of threw together a budget like last year's. Here it is. It isn't much and it won't take much to meet it."

On the other hand, here's the type of speech that causes people to stand up and take notice: "Your pastor and elders together have been earnestly seeking God's will for our ministry, and we feel this is going to be a key year. We have the opportunity to do something truly significant through this congregation, and we're eager to enlist your aid. Our vision for this church will require dedication and sacrifice from every one of us, and it is reflected in our newly revised budget for next year...."

One mood is weak and defeating; the other, strong and courageous. It's obvious which will inspire confidence and harvest a better response. People will give to something; they will give nothing much when the project appears to be nothing much.

Thus the first task of a successful stewardship campaign is to forge a compelling vision of what the congregation will be challenged to accomplish. Such a vision ought to have several characteristics:

- *Boldness.* Mild doesn't inspire. Mild isn't befitting a great God. Mild doesn't work. A holy boldness, however, moves people to response. The church leaders have already determined their priorities in writing the budget. This is the place to speak them boldly and confidently, while refraining from shallow hype.
- *Biblical integrity.* The bold vision must, of course, match God's will. It should be attached to the major imperatives in the Bible—the Great Commission, the great commandment, the building of the kingdom, the care and nurture of the saints. A vision to have "the largest parking lot in the county" or "to outgrow the Baptists" or to do anything else that smacks of empire building ought to be avoided.
- *Backing.* If the vision is something only the pastor has seen (perhaps in a dream after eating spicy pizza before bedtime), if the church leaders aren't enthusiastically behind it, if people have a hard time warming up to it, it's probably only a fancy rather than a vision. A genuine vision will be compelling; people will naturally want to buy in. It generates its own backing.
- *Broad doability.* To inspire giving, a vision must be concrete enough to be understood and reasonable enough to be believed. Yes, "Every saint mature!" might be a vision, but can people wrap their minds around what it means? Yes, God may be calling a fifty-member church to send teams to

evangelize all of Honduras, but probably not entirely within the next six months. A vision ought to pull people along toward a place they wouldn't necessarily be without it, but it can't be so esoteric or overwhelming that it loses people.

Some churches choose a single theme to be a rallying cry for the year, such as "The Year of Missions" or "Building the Foundation." This highlights the major thrust that will make the year and the budget stand out from others. Some churches focus on people—a new staff member to bring on that year, a missionary who will receive greater support, moving to a full-time pastor from a tent-maker. Some churches highlight something already happening successfully in the church and point out how giving has made this happen and will expand it in the next budget year.

Whatever churches do to create a compelling vision, they know it will bring better results than when there is no vision, and the default stewardship cry is "Just like last year, only slightly diminished!"

A Concrete Plan

Okay, now how are the people going to be approached to register their support of the compelling vision? Churches employ a number of methods. The old standby *every-member canvass* still serves well those churches that can actually find people home. Its personal attention and human touch have produced excellent results over the years. Another version uses a sort of chain letter, carried from one pledger to the next; the one visited makes a pledge and then becomes the visitor, carrying the material to the next party.

It is not uncommon for churches that once used one of these methods to have changed to another. The chief reason behind the switch is the changing social expectations in our day. Social calling is not common anymore, and catching people at home, getting through security, and even finding a warm welcome are not assured. In addition, churches that don't have a regular visitation program for shut-ins or inactives hesitate to make the only call some people receive in a year to be a solicitation for a pledge.

Telephone canvassing is used in some churches. A positive factor is that although people often are away from their phones, the preponderance of answering machines means the message can be delivered anyway. A negative factor these days is that people have become so pestered with phone solicitations by businesses and charities that they may resent their church joining the list of disturbers.

Some churches use a series of desserts or coffees, both at church and in people's homes. Members are invited, told what the purpose of the meeting is, entertained, briefed on the stewardship program, and given a commitment opportunity. This method has the advantage of being warm and personal and it even promotes fellowship. In a large church, however, logistics prove daunting because of the number of events and many repetitions of the message. The quality of events and the content of the message may vary greatly, depending on the varied leadership. In addition, this method doesn't reach persons who avoid or cannot attend a gathering.

Still other methods involve enlisting a corps of volunteers to handwrite notes to the congregation. Or a church may have a major banquet, fattening up the prospects for the appeal part of the program. Some pastors especially groom the "tribal chiefs" to get their precampaign support, and once word gets out that these opinion leaders are behind the campaign, the others follow happily. The methods are many; a concrete plan is behind each.

Some churches employ a mixture of print, group, and personal solicitation. Every person receives a stewardship package in the mail, containing, typically, (1) a flier or other materials showing budget highlights and explaining the budget and the vision that produced this blueprint for ministry, (2) a letter from the pastor or stewardship head inviting people to prayerfully respond to God's leading by pledging, (3) a pledge card and envelope to be placed in the offering plate or mailed back to the church, and (4) instructions on how to fill in the pledge card, often with charts showing figures for a tithe or proportional giving, or information about the number of pledges in various dollar-amount ranges given the previous year.

The printed material is supplemented with announcements in the bulletin or church newsletter. The pastor often preaches about stewardship and the compelling vision the leaders are placing before the congregation. Informational meetings may be held for people wanting to know more. A date is set for receiving the pledges, and persons not pledging (especially those who normally pledge) may receive a friendly reminder call a couple of weeks later. These calls often have the added benefit of finding out congregational-care needs that may have slipped through the cracks.

Plans such as these have served congregations well over the years. Customs change as people do, and what worked in one generation probably needs to be reworked in a new generation. Soliciting by targeted e-mail appeals—church "spam"—is probably just around the corner.

Baby Boomers have different habits and preferences from their aging parents' generation, which debuted many of the fund-raising techniques now in use. Boomers aren't particularly institutionally oriented and need to be convinced viscerally that a cause is worth supporting. The Busters (or Generation X) born 1961 to 1981 usually like anything the more numerous Boomers don't, just to be different. They are much more individualistic. Churches are finding some Busters heading toward churches out of a crying need for something to believe. Busters may prove to be more traditional than Boomers, but sadly, many need to be taught to give. Their parents didn't do it.

Whoever the target audience, the key to reaching them is a concrete plan engineered to move people from spectators or receivers to participants and givers.

Clear Communication

Essential to a concrete plan is clear communication to make known the compelling vision. God's people deep down want to give. They enjoy the sense of doing right and doing well. They believe in what they're doing and value their church. What they need is clear communication about the vision, the budget, the needs, and the nuts and bolts of giving. Several stewardship aspects demand clear communication:

- *The compelling vision.* How tragic for the church leaders to develop a terrific vision but fail to communicate it to the congregation! The vision often is most compelling as it comes to the congregation from the heart and hand of the pastor in sermon and written communications.
- *How funds are used and safeguarded.* No one wants to pour money into a leaky purse. One of the fastest

ways to dry up giving is to allow the impression to stand that the offerings are being used frivolously or fraudulently. Stewardship materials and year-long communications need to assure the congregation that their gifts are being spent with integrity and for worthwhile purposes. Stories of the effects of church expenditures, anecdotes from those helped, and information about board spending decisions provide givers with the assurances the church is using their money with the same care they give to its donation.

- *Proportional giving and tithing.* Many people, especially those new to church life, have little comprehension of the scale of church finances. Out of a culture that pays for its services, they dutifully drop a few dollars in the plate, generally in payment for the benefits received, as they would for a pay-what-you-can theater presentation. Many don't know—no one has instructed them—about biblical-theological reasons for giving. Nor do they understand all that the church does and thus needs help in doing.

The concept of *proportional giving* must be clearly communicated. It must be taught that it is not the amount of the gift that matters but the proportion of it, relative to what we spend on other things. Just where does *God* fit in our hierarchy of priorities, and does the proportion of our income given to God's work reflect our intentions? It cannot be assumed that people in general or even church members understand that concept, for they give nickels and dimes from a gold-plated lifestyle.

The tithe is another concept sorely in need of explanation. Coming out of an agrarian society, the concept of a tithe is lost on this generation.

First, there must be clarity of definition: A tithe is a *tenth* of *what?* If it represents the firstfruits, it is a tenth of gross, pretax income. In the Bible, if one got ten bushels from the field, the first went to God without regard to overhead. It was his. Period. And above that, one might give offerings.

Second, there must be clarity of explanation. In our day, with government taking over much of the responsibility for social welfare, it could be debated that our taxes pay for what part of the tithe was intended to do. When people pay taxes and when they give to parachurch organizations—is that figured in a tithe, or should the entire tithe go to the church for distribution? And are New Testament people required to tithe? Is it a requirement or only a measuring device (which by all rights ought to be bettered by thankful recipients of the New Covenant)? Each church needs to wrestle with those questions, but every church needs to educate the flock about the tithe and move people toward it as at least a beginning measure of Christian faithfulness in stewardship.

- *The meaning and mechanics of a pledge.* Conscientious people are wary of making a promise they're not sure they can keep. They need clear communication on the meaning of a pledge (a promise to give a certain amount regularly), why it is being asked of them (to encourage their faithful giving and the church's responsible planning and spending), what happens if their circumstances change (they can simply let the church know if they need to decrease their commitment, and they can always give more!), and how to write out the pledge and deliver it appropriately.
- *Exactly where the money will go.* An overview of the budget suits this communication well. Often

churches highlight special new initiatives or new spending. People appreciate knowing the agencies that will benefit from church benevolences, the programs and staff supported, the people helped, the denominational structures maintained. They have every right and reason to be well-informed through clear communication.

Assessing Effectiveness

When the pledge cards return, even the final few hounded out of the slow responders, the financial picture unfolds. Everyone is curious: What's the pledge total? Did we make budget? Actually, the total amount pledged is but one of the factors to assess. The expected pay-up percentage and sources of new money should also be considered.

Total Amount Pledged

Of course the pledge total is significant. The budget expects an income figure for pledges and is balanced around that amount. Did the stewardship drive produce pledges at least as great as the hoped-for income from pledges? Blessed is the church where this is the case! If the pledged amount is significantly lower than expected, the budget needs to be reworked, as was described in the previous chapter. If the pledges come in over budget, the church can rebudget to spend more, reserve more, or give more.

Pay-up Percentage

A little financial history can advise the church about pledge pay up. In past years did people generally give what they had pledged to give, or does the church actually need to receive pledges for a few percentage points above the budgeted amount to allow for anticipated slippage? Or maybe people actually give more than they pledge to give, and that can be anticipated in the budget.

It will take until the end of the year to know the exact pay-up percentage. It's a good figure to know. It helps with the following year's budgeting process, but of even greater value is the information pay up gives about member satisfaction—or maybe the local economy. People will often vote with their pocketbook, and if they dislike church spending or feel uninvolved, disfranchised, or ill informed, they will simply not meet their pledge. People being transferred or moving, people losing their jobs or retiring, people whose economic situation changes—all these factors help explain a low pay-up rate.

New Money

This is not redesigned bills or silver dollars. *New money* is a useful term for increased income derived from two categories of pledges: (1) new pledges from those who have not pledged before, plus (2) the increase from continuing pledges, less the decrease from pledges that shrank or were discontinued from the previous year. Seasoned financial eyes pay close attention to the new money figure, for it tells the amount of pledged income that is a true increase over the previous year.

If much of the new money is coming from new pledges, one of two things is happening: Either the church is gaining committed new people, or people who formerly contributed without pledging have begun to pledge instead. Either is a good sign for the vitality of the church.

If it is true that a number of former contributors have started pledging, however, and new contributors aren't taking their place, church leaders may find that their joy in the increased pledge income is somewhat offset by dismay over a decrease in the contributions income. It's possible that giving has remained nearly static, but the place the income shows up has changed because more givers have made a pledge. This is a common occurrence when churches make a big, new push for pledges. Churches in such a situation may need to decrease the budget figure for expected income from contributions to avoid a surprise later in the year.

If a large portion of the new money is coming from increased pledges and few people are decreasing or dropping their pledge, this indicates increased commitment and support on the part of continuing pledgers. Again, this is a sign of the effectiveness of church life as a whole and the stewardship emphasis in particular.

Celebrating Stewardship

One year I took the church youth group to Fourth of July fireworks on the beach in California. We told everyone how fun it would be. We wrote it up in the youth flier. We gathered at the beach and roasted marshmallows. This was going to be great! Then the fog rolled in. What we saw that evening was a random set of faint glows in the thick fog.

That should not be the experience of the congregation following the big buildup of a stewardship campaign. After the flurry of activity, publicity, and appeals, people deserve more than random faint glows of follow-up information. They need an opportunity to hear what their promises have provided. Does the vision written into the budget appear to be possible through the giving promised? Did the pledges meet or exceed expectations? Did pledges take an upward jump this year? Announce it at the least; celebrate it if at all possible.

A potluck celebration of thanks might be in order or a midyear pat on the back or a "Minute for Mission" in worship or an occasional series of vignettes illustrating the results of church giving. In fact stewardship should be a year-round program rather than a fall flurry. As the church lives through the year being supported by the budget, word of the pledgers' faithfulness would regularly be welcomed. That choir concert people so enjoyed? It's possible because of your giving. That successful vacation Bible school? It wouldn't have happened without the budgeted resources. As people see and appreciate the fruit of their giving, they realize once again that their decision to pledge was a good one and they will gladly do it again.

Raising money just got easier—and more enjoyable.

For Further Reading

Berkley, James D., ed. *Handbook of Management and Administration*. Grand Rapids: Baker, 1997. Useful articles on planning stewardship and special offerings.

Chaffee, Paul. *Accountable Leadership: Resources for Worshipping Communities*. San Francisco: ChurchCare Publishing, 1993. Good words on proportional giving.

Cunningham, Richard B. *Creative Stewardship*. Nashville: Abingdon, 1979. Talks about why people should give.

Holck, Manfred Jr. *Church Finance in a Complex Economy*. Nashville: Abingdon, 1983. Long a favorite guru on church finances, Manfred Holck provides creative ideas.

Receiving
and Recording Money

Assuming the planning, budgeting, and stewardship campaign went well, the time comes when the church actually begins to receive people's tithes and offerings for a given budget year. Thus begins the major responsibility of handling the income with security and accounting for it with accuracy.

The bulk of most churches' income arrives through the traditional Sunday offering. In the service of worship, as a response to God's love, people return to God their gifts of gratitude. The offering remains a vital, almost sacramental, element of worship, because it provides a tangible way to respond to the conviction of the preached Word and the experience of the Lord's Supper.

People love to joke about the offering: A plane is going down, and someone calls on a clergyperson to "do something religious," so he takes an offering. Sometimes worship leaders appear almost apologetic about taking an offering, as if it were a troublesome necessity rather than a gracious opportunity. Yet, for those who love the Lord and are excited about God's work in their midst, the offering provides a grand opportunity for unbottling the religious devotion they feel. Giving to God through the church to further God's work near and far—that's a holy privilege! With boldness and joy should an offering be taken.

Out of deference to seekers who come to church but don't necessarily understand the culture, some churches have modified or even eliminated the taking of an offering. A gracious preface is often added to the collection: "If you are new to this church or not yet a believer, please feel free *not* to participate in the collection we are about to take. We believe that Christians bear the responsibility of supporting the church and we don't want our guests to feel compelled in any way." Such a disclaimer demonstrates both hospitality and good theology. It also derails the cheap notion that "churches are just out to get your money."

Other churches never mention an offering during the service, but instead place receptacles at the door where the faithful are able to deposit their offering unobtrusively on the way out. Such a practice quietly allows for the believers to support their church without making the taking of an offering a central element of the service. Newcomers and seekers thus feel absolutely no pressure to give, which probably deflates some common prejudices they may have about the organized church.

But do such neophytes also lose out on an opportunity to learn about a key aspect of faith and discipleship? And does the downplay of such a central act of obedience somehow communicate that Christian stewardship is the church's dirty little secret rather than its grand privilege? These are questions for each church's leadership to wrestle with as they determine what is most faithful within their church culture.

No matter how money comes into the church's care, however, it needs to be handled in a safe and businesslike manner. Stolen or misallocated funds never get to produce the good they were given to accomplish. Banks have tellers' cages and fail-safe procedures to receive money; stores have cash registers and multiple levels of supervision. Churches, all too often, have Agnes with a deposit bag and a sharp pencil.

Let's examine how we might improve on the Agnes method of money handling, keeping in mind the internal controls introduced in chapter 2.

Safeguarding the Offering

Whether it is received in bags or plates, whether the receptacles come to the people or the people march to the receptacles, the way the offering is received in church provides an acceptable level of security through how publicly it is done. Somebody could conceivably swipe a twenty out of the plate as it is passed, but it's not likely to happen without being seen.

But once the plates are assembled in the back, *then* what happens to them? Typically the many offering plates get dumped into one or two plates. Sometimes the full plates head to a room to be counted or to a safe depository. Sometimes they are marched to the front for a prayer of dedication and spend the rest of the service on the communion table in plain sight. It's when the full plates are taken somewhere out of sight that special care is needed. They should, while still unsecured, always be in the care of at least two persons not from the same family. That means that if usher Loretta would like to make some of the loose change hers, usher Bill is there to keep the temptation in line.

It is simply prudent that at no time should the plates sit unwatched in the back of the church, on an office desk, or in the hands of only one person. Churches receiving the offering through receptacles at the door ought to have a person assigned to keep an eye on each receptacle so that it doesn't get dipped into or walk away.

The accumulated offering sitting somewhere in the church presents a great temptation to thieves who love to hit churches on Sunday night, thinking there's lots of money to be found. If the church has a very secure safe—floor safes are best—it may be okay to leave the money overnight. Better is an immediate count and deposit of the funds in a bank drop box. If an immediate count is not feasible, the entire offering should be deposited in a bank, to be picked up and counted on Monday. Under no circumstances should cash be taken from the uncounted offering to pay bills or reimburse expenses, nor should the money simply be locked in a church file cabinet or the treasurer's desk.

Counting the Offering

It is best to count the offering in a secure room behind locked doors. At least two trusted, careful individuals, neither of whom is the church treasurer who keeps the books, should do this job. Often church deacons, Finance Committee members, or retired persons with finance experience volunteer on rotating teams under the supervision of a staff member or church officer. To avoid collusion or the appearance of it, it is best not to staff a counting team with persons related to each other. Since persons on the counting teams will handle normally confidential information, such as what individuals give, they need to understand and abide by a strict code of confidentiality. With rotating teams, no one team knows all about everyone's giving, which is a benefit.

When the team emerges from the room, having done their job, the treasurer needs some specific information from them: (1) How much was given? (2) Who gave what? and (3) Where was the money directed? To answer those questions, two forms help keep the counting and reporting organized.

The first form—we'll call it the Contributions Form—is like a journal of sorts, listing the donors down the left side and providing a series of columns in which to record each donor's contributions to the various funds—general, building, missions, and so on. This form helps the counters credit the donors for their giving, allocates the giving according to the donors' wishes, and provides the information for a receipt to be given to each donor.

Figure 4
Contributions Form
Church of the Open Books

Date _____ Counters _____

Donor	Total	General	Building	Missions	Other
Chapman	$ 65.00	$ 50.00		$ 15.00	
Robinson	$ 200.00	$ 150.00	$ 25.00		$ 25.00 (Camp)
Woods	$ 45.00	$ 30.00	$ 5.00	$ 5.00	$ 5.00 (Xmas)
Loose plate	$ 213.45	$ 213.45			
Totals	$ 523.45	$ 443.45	$ 30.00	$ 20.00	$ 30.00

The second form—let's name it the Funds Form—provides a place for the various means of contribution (coins, paper, and checks) to be listed and for the various fund totals to be given. With this form, the counters transmit data to the treasurer for posting to the books.

Figure 5
Funds Form
Church of the Open Books

Money Count

Type	Sunday Amount	From the Week	Total
Coin	$ 13.45		$ 13.45
Paper	$ 55.00	$ 20.00	$ 75.00
Checks	$435.00		$435.00
Total	$503.45	$ 20.00	$523.45

Funds to Be Credited

Fund	Amount
General	$443.45
Building	$ 30.00
Missions	$ 20.00
Other	
Camp	$ 25.00
Xmas	$ 5.00
Total	$523.45

Counted by: _____ (signature)

_____ (signature)

_____ (signature)

_____ (signature)

Date of deposit: _____ **by** _____

Now, back inside the locked room, the counting team has the weekly offering to process. Often they also have accumulated donations that have arrived by mail or in person during the week, which they may process separately or treat as if they had come in on Sunday. Here's the procedure.

First, since loose cash is the most worrisome of income, the loose offering should be counted and placed in a bag or envelope for deposit. The "loose plate" total is recorded on the Contributions Form.

Unless the church board has stipulated otherwise, the loose cash will be credited to the general fund.

Second, loose checks are counted and credited to the donor's record on the Contributions Form. The loose checks are considered given to the general fund unless something else is stipulated on the check's memo line or the church has made other arrangements for a special offering (such as the Christmas Eve offering going to the hungry). Since loose-plate checks can be attributed to specific contributors, they are *not* added to the "loose plate" figure, but instead are recorded on the Contributions Form in sums by the names of donors. The loose checks are then temporarily set aside.

Third, offering envelopes are opened, and the cash or check contained in each is checked against the amount written by the donor on the envelope. If nothing is written on the envelope, the counter marks the correct amount. The envelopes are retained, to be given to the treasurer as a written verification of the amount given. The amount is listed on the Contributions Form. If the envelopes allow for a particular fund to be stipulated, the counter is careful to write the amount in that fund's column on the Contributions Form.

Fourth, now the table holds loose cash and loose checks counted and set aside, along with the contents—both cash and checks—of the offering envelopes. The Contributions Form ought to show a total, but the next task is to count and register on the Funds Form all of the cash, the paper currency, and the checks. This also helps prepare the offering for deposit in the bank. The total from this count ought to match the total on the Contributions Form. If it does, the counters are nearly done. If not, the source of the discrepancy needs to be found and corrected.

Fifth, it's time to wrap up the operation. The counters prepare the deposit slip to accompany the offering to the bank. Figures on the deposit slip need to be the same as those on the Funds Form. Then the counters individually verify the figures on all the forms and sign the Funds Form to show their concurrence with the count's numbers.

Cash, currency, and checks are bundled into a deposit bag and taken to the bank for immediate deposit. Since a number of people concur on the amount to be deposited and the treasurer's Funds Form records the amount, the person(s) depositing the money cannot short the deposit without being caught. It is prudent, however, to consider the safety of those making the deposit. In some neighborhoods if the amount is large, the security of the persons as well as the money ought to be a major concern.

The opened offering envelopes and forms are given to the treasurer, who can then post the income to the proper funds and update donor records. With this, the count is complete for another week.

New Ways to Receive Money

Where yesterday's church may have received offerings that included a chicken or a bag of beans, today's church has new options available for how money arrives. As people become accustomed to a nearly cashless society, more and more of their expenses are being put on plastic. Some churches, to accommodate people's desires, have arranged to receive contributions through credit cards. People using their cards to build up air miles or benefit another charity appreciate being able to charge their tithe to their account.

The church loses about 3 percent in transaction fees, but making the convenience available to donors may be worth it.

Churches have also gotten on the automatic withdrawal bandwagon. Just as people pay their monthly mortgage or utility bills by automatic withdrawal, so they can pay their tithe. With minimal paperwork, the church and donor can arrange for a given amount to be withdrawn from a donor's bank account each month and deposited in the church's account. The donor avoids the hassle of writing checks and remembering to take the offering envelope to church, and the church has the steady reliability of a monthly deposit. There's no problem with pledge payup with these folks unless they overdraw their bank account. Whenever donors change their pledges, a new automatic withdrawal arrangement can be made. Again, churches lose 2–3 percent of each transaction to bank fees but may consider it worthwhile, especially in August, when the automatic transaction doesn't go on vacation.

With the explosion of computers hooked up to the Worldwide Web, it is only a matter of time before people will be able to make a fund transfer to their church by the click of a mouse. Personal finance programs and bank tie-ins on the Web are becoming more sophisticated. In no time a "church mouse" will be the one whose click registers an electronic transfer from a donor's account to the church's.

Keeping the Books

If churches had only one fund to track, bookkeeping would be a piece of cake, but most churches have several funds to keep in balance. If everyone donated to their church with no preference whatsoever as to how the money should be spent, again, the bookkeeper would have an easier time. But many funds and designated giving keep church treasurers on their toes.

There is nothing particularly peculiar about church books. In a small- to medium-sized church, anyone with a head for figures, a little time, and a bit of training can learn to keep the books. Larger churches will require greater sophistication and education, most likely found in a paid staff member with accounting training and experience.

Powerful and user-friendly financial software has transferred much bookkeeping today from a bound journal with hand entries onto a computer screen and pages of printouts. Smaller churches can modify personal or small-business versions of such computer programs as Quicken or Microsoft Money to keep their books. Larger churches will probably want to use more specialized programs provided especially for churches and tied to database programs. A number of vendors offer church financial programs and user support.

Computers are wonderful tools, but when software is chosen poorly or used clumsily, a computer can compound errors and frustration at an amazing clip. Care must be taken to choose an appropriate program, insure competent use of the program, and customize the program to produce useful and effective reports rather than reams of financial "noise" that no one understands. In addition, computer security becomes especially important when sensitive records are kept there.

Whether by hand or by computer, a bookkeeper needs to keep up to date what amounts to a number of lists and sums. These records provide the information church leaders need to make sound decisions.

The *journal* is the key document. A journal keeps track of what money is coming in and where it is going. Income is listed on the journal as credits; expenses are listed as debits. The bottom line tells you how much you have—or don't have—as the case may be. Separate journals can be kept for each of the church funds, but more often one journal is kept, with the funds being reflected in columns on the journal. When people maintain their checkbooks properly, they are keeping an elementary journal, with entries of money coming in (deposits) and money going out (checks written), and the resultant balance.

All of a church's transactions need to end up in the journal. Thus, once the counters give the bookkeeper the Contributions Form, the bookkeeper needs to make journal entries to account for that income. Other income deriving from interest on savings accounts, rent, or whatever other source also gets posted to the journal. Accuracy in transferring figures, precision in posting to the correct funds, and attention to detail serve a bookkeeper well. While most pastors and other leaders don't need to know the details of accounting, a general understanding of the principles allows them to provide oversight, ask intelligent questions, and use the answers knowledgeably.

Reporting Useful Information

Any bookkeeper with a computer printer can crank out reams of financial reports. A *good* bookkeeper will produce reports that have useful, meaningful, appropriate data that keep church leaders informed without drowning them in inexplicable numbers. Legion are the pastors and board members who receive a financial report only to stare bewilderedly at it and wonder if they are the only fools who don't understand it! Welcome is the report that bears financial information in a user-friendly format.

Pastors and other leaders usually need to master only a few reports: the balance sheet, the income statement, the income statement with comparisons, and the general ledger.

The Balance Sheet

The balance sheet gives a snapshot of the current fiscal state of the organization. A balance sheet typically lists assets on one side and liabilities on the other. The assets include such items as cash in the bank, property, buildings, furnishings, supplies, and accounts receivable (what is owed the church). Liabilities, on the other side, include accounts payable (what the church owes, such as back rent or bills due at a stationery store), and unpaid loan balances. Subtract liabilities from assets, and you get the *fund balance.*

Frankly, financial whizzes, lending institutions, and auditors show great interest in balance sheets. Pastors, deacons, and elders often fail to see the point. Generally speaking, if the net assets are greater than the previous year, the church is probably staying above water financially.

The Income Statement

Now *here's* something a pastor wants to know! An income statement reports the income, expenses, and net income (or loss) over a given period. Is the money that's coming in taking care of the expenses being paid? An income statement reveals the answer.

At least every month and then at year-end, all eyes turn toward the income statement. How did offerings hold up during the summer? Has the Youth Department kept expenses down? We're short on cash, so which departments have been overspending? We paid *what* for electricity in February? Are we in the black or in the red? Look at the income statement.

The income statement can be detailed, giving figures for each line item in the budget, or it can summarize the information on one page, providing totals for categories and departments. Pastors and boards can decide how exhaustive they want their report, but an income statement needs to be *complete,* providing (in detail or summary) all the income and expenses for the period. Nothing hidden. No surprises.

Figure 6
February Income Statement—General Fund
Church of the Open Books

Income

Pledges	$4,000
Contributions	$1,500
Loose Plate	$ 550
Interest	$ 50
Rent	$ 400
Total Income	$6,500

Expenses

Personnel	$3,000
Program	$ 600
Facilities*	
Debt payment	$ 300
Electricity	$1,000
Other utilities	$ 0
Insurance	$ 200
Cleaning	$ 200
Benevolences	$1,000
Total Expenses	$6,300
Net Income	$ 200

*This category expanded for illustrative purposes.

Income Statement with Comparisons

Of even greater utility than the income statement alone is the income statement that contains added data, such as last year's (or month's) comparable figures, or how this period's figures compare to the amounts expected when the budget was drawn up and cash flows figured. Many income statements have columns not only for the given month but also for year-to-date figures.

For example, the chair of Building and Grounds gets the February income statement and looks at the cost of electricity. It's $1,000! Is that good or bad? Well, what did the church spend for electricity in January of this year, or last February? A comparison income statement will include comparison figures that go beyond just the facts and provide information for analysis.

The B&G chair may also want to know how that $1,000 compares to how much the church budgeted for electricity. Is it more than expected? Sophisticated comparison income statements include the expected monthly figure from the cash flow budget, thus allowing the chair to compare what the church actually spent with what it expected to spend. Year-to-date figures on the income statement show how much of the yearly budget has been expended.

All this information helps those with spending powers analyze how well they are doing in matching spending to income or spending to expectations. The income and expense figures stand beside relevant data that help the church leaders interpret those figures.

The General Ledger

The general ledger lists all the income and expenses by account number, item by item. This is especially use-

Figure 7
February Income Statement—General Fund
Church of the Open Books

Account	Feb 1998	Jan 1998	Feb 1997	Feb Expct	YTD	YTD 1997	YTD Expct	Annual Budget
Income								
Pledges	$ 4,000	$ 4,100	$ 3,800	$ 3,900	$ 8,100	$ 7,700	$ 7,900	$55,000
Contributions	$ 1,500	$ 1,450	$ 1,400	$ 1,400	$ 2,950	$ 2,800	$ 2,900	$18,000
Loose Plate	$ 550	$ 560	$ 570	$ 500	$ 1,110	$ 1,700	$ 1,050	$ 6,500
Interest	$ 50	$ 48	$ 40	$ 50	$ 98	$ 78	$ 100	$ 600
Rent	$ 400	$ 400	$ 400	$ 400	$ 800	$ 800	$ 800	$ 4,800
Total Income	$ 6,500	$ 6,558	$ 6,210	$ 6,250	$13,058	$13,078	$12,750	$84,900
Expenses								
Personnel	$ 3,000	$ 3,000	$ 2,800	$ 3,000	$ 6,000	$ 5,600	$ 6,000	$36,000
Program	$ 600	$ 500	$ 600	$ 700	$ 1,100	$ 1,200	$ 1,000	$14,000
Facilities*								
Debt payment	$ 300	$ 300	$ 300	$ 300	$ 600	$ 600	$ 600	$ 3,600
Electricity	$ 1,000	$ 200	$ 250	$ 275	$ 1,200	$ 450	$ 475	$ 2,000
Other utilities	$ 0	$ 300	$ 325	$ 350	$ 300	$ 675	$ 650	$ 2,500
Insurance	$ 200	$ 0	$ 175	$ 200	$ 200	$ 175	$ 200	$ 400
Maintenance	$ 200	$ 175	$ 150	$ 175	$ 375	$ 300	$ 350	$ 2,100
Benevolences	$ 1,000	$ 1,000	$ 950	$ 1,000	$ 2,000	$ 1,900	$ 2,000	$24,300
Total Expenses	$ 6,300	$ 5,475	$ 5,550	$ 6,000	$11,775	$10,900	$11,275	$84,900
Net Income (Loss)	$ 200	$ 1,083	$ 660	$ 250	$ 1,283	$ 2,178	$ 1,475	$ 0

*This category expanded for illustrative purposes.

ful for pinpointing troubling facts or good news, or for correcting errors.

To again use the B&G chair: Suppose that after comparing February's $1,000 charge for electricity, the chair still considers it suspiciously high. She can ask the bookkeeper for a report on the electricity account number from the general ledger. She should receive a listing of the items charged to that account. For February there ought to be one electricity bill paid to the utility company. But aha! The chair finds that not only that bill, but also the water, sewer, garbage, and Bible bookstore bills were charged in error to the electricity account. There's the problem.

Remember the general ledger. It's the church leader's route to tremendously useful information.

Sending Receipts to Donors

The weekly Contributions Form that the bookkeeper uses to post receipts provides the information for a bookkeeping responsibility not only suggested by accountants, not only taught by mothers everywhere, but also required by law for donors to obtain tax benefits: receipts that report to donors what they have given. What? Your mom didn't make you send receipts, you say? Well, how about thank-you notes for gifts received—she taught you well, didn't she?

Receipts—sometimes called *giving statements*—mailed to donors provide a number of functions:

- *Compliance with the Tax Law of 1993.* For donors to obtain the tax benefits of charitable contributions, they need verification of their gifts to the church. To be claimed, any gift over $250 requires a receipt. An annual or quarterly statement of giving from the church fulfills this requirement. It should be stated somewhere on the receipt that "no tangible benefit was received by the donor in exchange for the contribution." (*Tangible* is the key word here; the IRS just doesn't understand spiritual benefits!)

- *A review of counting and posting accuracy.* When a donor receives an annual or quarterly statement of his or her giving, the church's record ought to coincide with the donor's record. Let's say you make a habit of placing two $10 bills in your offering envelope each week. Whenever he's on the counting team, however, Avaricious Al slips one into his pocket and credits you with only a $10 contribution. When you get your statement, you see a number of weeks when your $20 contribution was posted as only $10. Now you can bring this up with your treasurer and something can be done. If Al had taken checks from your envelope and endorsed them to himself, you'd have an even stronger case.

- *An opportunity to sincerely thank those giving to the church.* Remember, we don't want enthusiastic donors to experience all hype and only a glimmer of response to their giving. With the receipts can go a warm letter of praise and thanks, informing the donor of the fruits of the giving.

- *A subtle reminder to bring a lagging pledge up to date.* Perhaps momentary sentiment stirred a pledge, but now day-to-day faithfulness in giving has lagged. Receiving a giving statement with a bunch of zeros on it or a haphazard donation pattern often will cause a delinquent donor to make a pledge current.

Auditing and Reviewing the Books

Anybody handling or accounting for tens of thousands of someone else's dollars needs somebody looking over his shoulder. It need not be suspicious oversight or adversarial, but it needs to happen in a number of ways to maintain accuracy and integrity.

- *General oversight.* Any time financial reports are produced, the church leadership in general bears the fiduciary responsibility to examine them. Persons responsible for their departments' budgets ought to take special interest in the accuracy of their sections of the report. In addition, someone in particular—the chair of the Finance Committee, the volunteer treasurer who doesn't keep the books or count the money but relays digested information to the board, the church business manager—someone ought to be made personally responsible for being a nitpicker. Reports made but not read or examined are useless.

- *Preliminary examinations.* Short of a sometimes-costly and involved external audit, a financial oversight committee can conduct auditlike inspections of the books. What a CPA would call a *compilation* of financial statements is a first-order service a volunteer accountant or third-party group can accomplish. Often a compilation prompts those responsible for bookkeeping to do more thorough record keeping. In a *review* a CPA spends time analyzing financial data and tracing sample transactions. It is nearly as rigorous as an audit. An *internal audit* utilizes a team of knowledgeable but disinterested parties from the church to perform much of what an external audit would do but without the cost and sterling credibility of a CPA firm. Internal auditors can use a thorough checklist similar to the procedures of an external audit team.

- *External audit.* For large churches, those going through transitions in financial personnel, those fearing or wanting to still suspicion of financial improprieties, those required by a lending institution or denomination, and those who want to be extra safe, an external audit provides the seal of accounting approval. For this several-thousand-dollar service, insist on a CPA. Note, however, that a full audit should not be solely relied on to detect fraud.

Blessing the Books

Whenever "all is safely gathered in," a church ought to give thanks to the Lord of the harvest, who provides all to those who give. It isn't just money the church receives and posts; it's blessings and commitment and hard work and sacrifice. The care given to these offerings honors both the givers and the ultimate Giver behind it all. And it preserves the gifts to be spent as intended.

For Further Reading

Berkley, James D., ed. *Handbook of Management and Administration.* Grand Rapids: Baker, 1997. Chapter 35 covers much of the same territory with a number of articles.

Busby, Daniel. *The Zondervan Church and Nonprofit Organization Tax and Financial Guide.* Grand Rapids: Zondervan, 2000. Full of cautions, ideas, and fine helps.

Tennyson, Mack. *Church Finances for People Who Count.* Grand Rapids: Zondervan, 1990. This is the simplest, most straightforward exposition of how to keep books.

Six

Spending Money

Bertrand Russell wrote, "To be without some of the things you want is an indispensable part of happiness." If this is so, churches ought to be wildly happy.

Any church, any committee of that church, any individual on that committee can easily expend the entire church budget—in their spare time, in a week, on but one benevolence. Available money is always a finite commodity; legitimate needs are always plentiful. So what's a church to do?

Actually the budget is a great place to start, and we've already worked out that tool. The key to spending church money prudently is to provide benevolent controls that keep the spending on target within the budget.

Notice the *benevolent* part. No faithful church volunteer or harried staff member should have to fight through a regulatory forest to breach the Fort Knox of church treasuries to accomplish the work of the church. A spending policy needs to be clear, convenient, and uncomplicated.

Notice also, however, the *controls* half of "benevolent controls." Without controls, spending quickly becomes foolish, extravagant, and untracked. Original sin teams up with confusion and miscommunication to create fiscal disaster.

What is needed is a plan.

Who Has Authority to Spend?

The church Agnes served as do-all treasurer kept a running bill at a corner grocery. Someone planning a youth event would dash in, pick up some popcorn, and say the magic words: "Put it on the church tab." Then a Ladies Aid member would buy cream and sugar for after-church coffees, a deacon would get a get-well card, and trustees would make several trips for picture-hanging hardware. All simply put the cost on the church bill, which Agnes paid monthly with church funds. I'm convinced practically anybody could have purchased their weekly groceries and just charged it to the church. The only control on that spending was the judgment of the store clerk. Obviously that's not the preferred method.

The church board needs to decide just who is authorized to approve expenditures and then put that decision into a policy statement. A small church may operate more like a family, with a handful of people given that responsibility, each staying current on the church's financial situation. When each is free to operate somewhat independently, however, frequent communication becomes essential. In midsize churches the responsibility probably will need to be more systematized. The board may want to provide approval authority to a number of staff members and key lay leaders, each with primary responsibility for a portion of the budget but with some overlapping authority to cover for others' periodic unavailability.

Large churches need to get downright business-like, with department heads and/or committee chairs charged with managing their portion of the budget or delegating someone to do it for them. Thus the choir director or committee chairperson, or his/her appointed designee, would need to sign off on any music purchases; the youth director or youth committee chair would have to approve Youth Department expenditures; and so on. With a point person for each section of the budget, the buck stops (and starts!) with an individual who both manages the accounts and can be held responsible if spending goes awry.

Each church will devise a different plan, but every church *needs* a plan. Too many cooks will not only spoil the soup; they'll probably empty the pot as well.

What Can Be Spent?

Let's say you're the one tapped to authorize spending for church vehicles. Obviously your authority is not unlimited. You wouldn't expect to be able to purchase a fleet of stretch BMWs for parking shuttles. So how much can you spend?

Look to the budget, particularly the portion dealing with church vehicles. You find you control a lease line item, one for repairs, and another for gas and oil. Now your authority has dimensions. But still, you need to know how the church regards the budget.

Specifically, is the budget intended to be a firm "You can spend no more than this!" limit, or is the budget meant to be a "This is our most accurate estimation of what it will cost" guideline that often gets overspent a little because it is set intentionally without any fluff? Churches use one kind of budgeting structure or the other, and you, as manager, need to know which to follow. Exceed your budget in the first case, and your head may roll. Consistently *underspend* your budget in the second case, and your estimating abilities are impugned. Wise is the manager who conforms to the kind of budget philosophy in play!

If the money is there in the budget, *should* it be spent? Those acquainted with bureaucracies know the use-it-or-lose-it syndrome. The temptation is to scramble to fully spend a budget item this year to justify equal or greater funding the next. This inevitably leads to poor spending decisions and outright waste.

Stewardship calls for a nobler plan. It is not a virtue to spend little or nothing of a budget, hoarding as cash what was meant to be converted into ministry. So it's no star in a manager's fiscal cap to end a year having bothered to spend little of a budget item deemed important enough to be funded originally. But neither is it good stewardship to spend madly, merely for the purpose of using up a line item before the budget year ends.

A good steward will manage a line item to spend it as needed and as is appropriate. When a new budget is formed, a wise church will reward such judicious stewardship with a line item that reflects the actual needs of the coming year, not merely the history of past spending.

Some approval mechanism is needed for expenditures beyond the budget. Even a well-planned budget cannot envision every eventuality. Who could guess the freak January freeze would crack the church van's engine block? Now that vehicle maintenance line item will be fully expended in January, so where will the maintenance money come from for the rest of the year?

Typically, an organization expects expenditures to come out close to the budgeted amounts. If an item like vehicle maintenance is going to blow the budget wide open, some person or board needs to know and approve the large deviation. A small variance might be absorbed by other line items in the group—gasoline, for instance, may be underspent—so that the group subtotal stays within bounds. Such a deviation usually is absorbed naturally without further need for approval.

Churches often build a contingency account into a budget as a cushion for unexpected large expenditures. Of course every budget manager can't use the contingency money like a personal slush fund. Typically the church business manager, the board, or the finance committee needs to approve the use of the contingency money to cover overruns.

Economic downturns, church splits, or overenthusiastic income projections may cause the actual income not to keep pace with expected income. Midyear budget adjustments are not uncommon in churches with vigilant fiscal watchers. Those tracking income may project a decrease in expected annual giving. The church can wait until December and throw their hands up in horror, or the leaders can decide to clamp down on spending until indicators pick up.

If the wisdom of the latter proactive action is chosen, all those approving expenditures have the collegial responsibility to be good soldiers and bear the lean months' discipline together. A mad scramble to snatch the remaining piece of the pie is conduct unbecoming a steward.

How Is Approval Communicated?

The people doing the buying and those approving the expenditures are not the ones cutting and signing the checks that pay for them. So what's the best way to transmit formal approval of church expenditures to the bill payers? Churches, like any business, need standard operating procedures.

In Agnes's church, pretty much anything went. A trustee might say, "Last night I told Agnes to expect a big bill tomorrow for the final payment on the reroofing job." This $10,000 shocker probably rocked the checking account. Or the flower committee would hand her a bill from a florist and just say, "Please pay it, Agnes. It's okay." The other extreme is the requirement to complete a notarized form in quadruplicate, signed in blood by five church officers and your mother, and verified by 8 x 10 glossies of the purchased item.

A *reasonable* plan might include the following instruments.

Purchase Order

Purchase orders are used by those *not* authorized to approve purchases and are signed by someone who is authorized to approve such expenditures. A purchase order is a form prepared by a buyer to describe the item to be bought.

Say I'm a Sunday school teacher and need a Bible dictionary for my classroom. I'm not one of the people who can authorize Christian education purchases, but I can fill out a purchase order for the book, have the Sunday school superintendent sign it and write in the "curriculum" account number, and give it to the treasurer. Then after I've put the book on the church's account at the Bible bookstore, a bill will come to the treasurer, who will use the purchase order to know the legitimacy of the charge and the account to charge it against.

Figure 8
Church of the Open Books
Purchase Order

Purchase Order Number: _____

Date: _____

Vendor: _____

Address: _____

Phone: _____ FAX: _____

Item	Quantity	Catalogue Number	Description	Charge to	Price
1					
2					
3					
4					
5					
6					
7					
8					
				Subtotal	
				Tax	
				Total	

Requested by: _____ Date: _____

Authorized by: _____ Date: _____

Check Request

The person who prepares church checks for signing is not intended to be someone of authority. It is a clerical role, and, for internal-control purposes, that person should not be able to authorize payment. Thus the check writer needs something in writing that says it is proper to produce a check on a certain account for a specified amount. That's the *check request form.*

The check request is filled out by the party desiring a check. Maybe it's a youth advisor wanting to rent an earth ball for the fall retreat. She writes in who the payee is, the amount, the date needed, whom to give the check to, and, if she knows it, the account to charge. Then that volunteer gets the associate pastor's signature (who manages the youth account and can supply the account number if the volunteer doesn't have it) and passes the check request to the check writer, who cuts the check, has it signed, and transmits it to the proper destination.

If the associate pastor wanted to initiate the check request for the earth ball, he would need to get the youth committee chair or maybe the senior pastor to sign his request. It is good internal-control policy on check requests for the requesting party not to be able to approve self-originated requests.

One more twist: Let's say the youth advisor was taking the youth group to Earth Ball World and planned for the church to pay admission. The problem is, she's not sure how many will show up. The solution? A *not-to-exceed check request.* For this check request, the advisor estimates no more than fifteen kids will show up at an admission cost of $3 per ticket. Then she requests a check not to exceed $50, to be safe. On authorization, this special check is issued with the amount blank and "not to exceed $50" inscribed prominently on the

Figure 9
Church of the Open Books
Check Request

Today's date: _____ Department: _____

Date for payment: _____ Check request #: _____

Budget accounts to be charged: _____ $ _____

_____ $ _____

_____ $ _____

TOTAL $ _____

Check payable to: _____

Send check to: _____

_____

_____

Purpose: _____

_____

Requested by: _____

Approved by: _____

(Business office only: Check #: _____)

face. When she gets to Earth Ball World, the advisor fills in the correct amount and keeps the carbon, which she promptly returns to the check writer on returning to church.

Invoice

Invoices are used by those empowered to approve expenditures. Although technically different, an invoice functions pretty much like a bill. The seller gives the buyer an invoice, which details the items purchased, the cost, and the method of shipping. If the associate pastor above decided to buy an earth ball, he could order it and ask to be billed. When the earth ball comes, the associate pastor can sign the accompanying invoice, write on it the account number to be charged, and pass it along to the church finance office for payment and accounting. Thus the bill payer knows the bill is legitimate, the merchandise has arrived, and the purchase is appropriately authorized.

Interfund-transfer Request

Interfund-transfer requests are used for internal adjustments of funds. When a church has a number of separate funds, sometimes one fund needs to pay another. That's when a transfer needs to be authorized through an interfund-transfer request. The request form authorizes the bookkeeper to make the adjustment.

For example, let's say the associate pastor above gets the monthly financial report and discovers his earth

Figure 10
Church of the Open Books
Fund Transfer Request

Date: _____ Amount: $_____

Transfer **from** account #: _____

Transfer **to** account #: _____

Person requesting transfer: _____

Purpose: _____

_____

Approved by: _____

ball was accidentally charged to the Foreign Missions account rather than the Youth account. He can instigate a correction through an interfund-transfer request, authorizing the correct amount to be taken out of the Youth account in the general fund and placed as a credit in the Foreign Missions account in the missions fund.

Or let's say the Advertising account was charged for a big ad in the local paper to invite youth to the Earth Ball World activity. When the Advertising account was set up to advertise worship, it wasn't planned to include this youth-related expense. Conversely, the Youth account had some extra dollars to use for outreach. The associate pastor could use an interfund-transfer request to replenish the Advertising account by reducing the Youth account.

How Are Items Paid?

Pay by check. It's best, for it leaves the kind of paper trail accountants cherish. Use cash mighty sparingly, and then only with verified authorization and documented receipting—and *never* from cash in the offering plate. With these two rules, only some scattered tips remain:

- *The check preparer should neither authorize nor sign the checks.* Internal control dictates that the one cutting the check does so only with proper authorization from another party and should never be given check-signature authority. When authorizing, writing, and signing checks remain in three different hands, temptation is practically eliminated.
- *Signature authority for checks should be established by the board.* The official ruling board should set the

standards for both who can sign checks and how many signatures are needed. In spite of convenience, the practice of having the pastor sign checks is highly discouraged by church finance authorities, because of internal-control problems involved with a check authorizer also being a check signer. The number of people authorized to sign checks should be kept small—perhaps two to four.

The number of signatures required is another board call. One signature is convenient but not secure. Two signatures on all checks is a safer procedure but impractical. Many churches require but one signature on checks for small amounts and two signatures for checks over a certain figure—set depending on the church's risk-comfort level. *Never* should blank checks be signed in advance by one party, since it completely defeats the purpose of requiring two signatures. Two signatures means two persons weigh the advisability of any major disbursement, and one person cannot singlehandedly enrich herself at the church's expense.

- *Nothing is paid without authorization and documentation.* A board can establish what it considers routine matters that don't require individual authorization. Most treasurers have blanket authorization to pay routine expenses covered by the budget, such as mortgage payments, utilities, and payroll. Other items require authorization, as explained above.

Documentation for expenses ought to become part of the record of every transaction—an *original* invoice (no copies to avoid duplicate payments) for bills, a check request for other payments, an annotated receipt for reimbursements. Even a written explanation is better than no documentation. An investigator should, at any point, be able to pull out of the files explanatory documentation for any check written.

- *Use checks appropriate for a business enterprise.* The family checkbook and check register are too meager for church use. A business-size check register is better because of the extra area for writing supporting information on the check stub. Checks should be used in strict order, and any checks voided need to be filed and accounted for. Computer software and printers add both security and convenience to check writing and thus are commonly used today.

- *Keep check writing contemporaneous.* In other words, don't write and postdate checks, hoping the funds will be there after the later date on the check. Don't write and hold checks, waiting for money to come in. Write checks when the money is in the account to cover them, and use the correct date.

Being Careful with Cash

Not *all* church transactions are by check. A precious few can be in cash through the *petty cash fund* and *cash advances.*

Petty Cash Fund

A *petty cash fund,* as the term implies, is used for small, random purchases that would be bothersome to pay by check. Somebody picks up Bic pens at the drugstore. The mail carrier wants 55 cents for postage due. Doughnuts are purchased for the staff birthday party. Each of these expenditures is legitimate, each with an account to be charged against. Paying from petty cash is the most efficient way to batch these small purchases into one check (as we will see).

A petty cash fund works like this: First, it should be a truly small amount of money. Twenty, fifty, one hundred dollars—not any more than the church can bear to lose. Second, the money needs to be placed in a relatively secure place, often a locking cash box that itself can be locked in a desk or cabinet.

Third, the fund should be placed in the care of a single individual. Only that one person ever gets into the petty cash box; only that person authorizes disbursements of cash and assures their documentation. Several people cannot keep the same till—even meticulous people—for if it ever is out of balance, no one knows who is responsible. The petty-cash guardian should be given a solid policy about what exactly petty cash can be used for, and be expected not to bend the rules.

Fourth, any disbursement from petty cash must be documented. If I get 55 cents for postage due, I need to sign and leave the 55-cent postage-due notice to replace the 55 cents in the cash box. I also need to write on that documentation the account number to be charged for my cash disbursement.

Fifth, at any given time, the actual cash in the box together with the sum of the documenting receipts must equal the beginning amount of cash. If the box started with $50 and my 55-cent postage due is the only disbursement, the 55-cent receipt should sit with $49.45 in cash.

Sixth, when the cash gets low, the guardian trades the accumulated receipts for a check for the same amount from the church treasurer. The guardian cashes the check, and that cash replenishes the petty-cash fund. If cash plus receipts previously equaled $50, now old cash plus new cash should still equal $50 in the box. The treasurer charges the amount of the new check against the accounts written on the receipts.

Cash Advance

Cash advances are a second way cash may occasionally be used in a church. A cash advance is entrusted to an individual with the understanding that it will be fully accounted for immediately following the need it is advanced to fill. Employee travel is a common reason for cash advances. Youth and children's programming may also require cash for admissions or unforeseen circumstances.

Let's say the church database whiz is being sent to a training conference in an adjoining state. She will need taxi and tip money, cash for food at the airport, airport van fare, and a few dollars just for security. The church advances her $100 for the trip. On the trip, she is careful always to keep a record and get a receipt where possible each time she spends some of the advance. She does not use the advanced cash for other purposes, nor does she use it back home for other church uses, such as to buy computer paper on sale. The cash is used only for the purpose it was advanced to fill.

When the database manager returns from her trip, she quickly turns in the remaining cash along with receipts and documentation for the cash spent. Returned cash plus documentation should equal the $100 advanced. This accounting for the advance needs to be done within days of her return to satisfy the IRS that the advance wasn't simply another way of giving her taxable income. The treasurer charges the appropriate accounts for the portion of the cash advance that the person used, and all is neatly wrapped up.

Cash advances should not be used when checks, not-to-exceed checks, church credit, billing, or other payment method is possible. It is for that rare occasion when only cash will work and the church doesn't want the employee or volunteer to have to use his or her own money and then be reimbursed. The church, instead, entrusts cash to the responsible party, who accounts for it promptly and fully.

Paying Employees

Half or more of many churches' disbursements go to employees as salaries and benefits. Much of payroll is rather routine and predictable when the workforce is stable. Pay period by pay period, a number of given tasks must be accomplished with precision and dispatch, because not only is people's livelihood at stake but also Uncle Sam takes more than a passing interest in the process. Mistakes in payroll cause much attention, and some can cause hefty penalties. So, to most employers, payroll is both routine and daunting at the same time.

Outside contractors known as *payroll services* can take some of the worry out of payroll administration for churches with complex personnel rosters or timid treasurers. The church supplies the information and funds to a payroll service, and the service prepares the payroll and writes the checks, taking their cut, of course. They also sweat the considerable paperwork required for withholding and government reports.

While working a church treasurer through the intricacies of preparing a payroll is beyond the scope of this book, there are a number of tips and caveats that those who manage a church will benefit from considering:

- *Churches must comply with most of the payroll and tax laws other employers must obey.* Some people think churches are charmed, Teflon-coated entities exempt from government regulation. Not at all. The noncompliant can be rudely awakened.

- *Someone in the church payroll structure needs to read and understand IRS Circular E (Publication 15).* This publication explains payroll withholding for employers, and compliance is more than suggested.
- *Treating church employees as independent contractors often is a mistake.* Few church workers are truly independent contractors, yet churches like to treat workers as such to save money. Get competent tax advice before considering a worker an independent contractor.
- *Pastors are considered self-employed for Social Security purposes and church employees for income-tax purposes.* This mixed classification makes clergy taxes a confusing proposition. Churches should *not* pay the government what would be the employer's share of FICA (Social Security) for a pastor, although they can give the pastor that amount as added salary to help the pastor pay the entire self-employment tax (SECA) amount. Churches *should* withhold and pay FICA for other employees. To complicate matters, generally a pastor's housing allowance isn't substantially taxable income for income-tax purposes but *is* entirely taxable for SECA purposes. Go figure.
- *Not all employee benefits are untaxed.* Many are untaxed, but not all. Churches may need legal advice when setting up pensions, health insurance, or "cafeteria plan" benefit packages for employees. Of special government concern is fairness for the lower-paid employees. Churches are excluded from COBRA requirements in relation to medical insurance.

- *Churches need to get an Employer Identification Number (EIN) for reporting purposes.* They also should get the customary W-4 from all employees and should issue W-2s to all employees before February 1 of a new year.
- *Churches must issue a 1099-MISC to persons who aren't church employees but are paid $600 or more in any given year.* Honoraria for speakers or musicians often accumulate to this amount in a year, so be sure to get Social Security numbers from all such payees.
- *Employees need to be paid for all hours worked.* Church employees tend to work "off clock" hours and overtime without expecting payment. The government, however, through the Fair Labor Standards Act (FLSA), expects payment for all hours worked. According to regulations, employees cannot volunteer time doing what they normally get paid to do. Not all churches are subject to FLSA regulations, but many are, and the rest may choose to be at least as fair with their employees.
- *Church officers may be held responsible to pay IRS non-compliance penalties personally!* That gets most pastors' attention.

Payroll can feel like a serious minefield for the uninitiated. That's sad, because the ability to provide meaningful labor and a Christian vocation to employees ought to feel more like a joyous privilege for the church as an employer and less like a perilous endeavor.

Reimbursing Employees

Church financial consultants agree that the preferred way for the church to shoulder the professional expenses of employees is an *accountable reimbursement plan*. In years past, pastors and many other church employees had sums called "expense allowances" tacked on to their paycheck. This money was intended to defray the costs of driving on ministry business, buying books, heading off for study leave, and other professional expenses that rightfully belong to the employer rather than the employee.

This old method must cease. Tax-law changes have rendered such a plan inadvisable, because when such nonaccountable allowances are paid outright, the government considers them just that much more taxable income to the employee. Deductions for professional expenses are largely lost.

The correct method is an *accountable* reimbursement plan. With this method, a reimbursement fund is designated in the budget for each eligible employee. When the employee incurs a professional expense, the employee submits documentation to a supervisor, who authorizes a reimbursement check paid by the church. Most churches reimburse employees up to a limit set in the budget. For tax reasons, employees should not be given the remainder of a reimbursement fund if money remains at the end of the year. Accountable reimbursements are not considered income for tax purposes and need not be reported to the IRS by the church.

Expense documentation needs to include five items: (1) the date, (2) the place (name of hotel, café, etc.), (3) the amount of the expense, (4) the person(s) involved, and (5) the ministry purpose. By adding names and ministry purpose to a printed receipt from a restaurant, tollway, parking garage, or other such establishment, an employee easily fulfills this requirement. "Ministry purpose" can be as brief a notation as "talked over youth policy" or "conducted annual review."

For car expenses, reimbursement for mileage requires that a contemporaneous record be kept of odometer readings; vague, "Oh, about 50 miles" reckonings aren't sufficient. Or meticulous record keepers can submit records of actual costs of operating the automobile (depreciation, maintenance, gas, repairs, insurance) and claim the portion of costs determined by ministry use of the car. Commuting miles are considered personal use and cannot be considered ministry expenses.

A corporate credit card is yet another way for the church to pick up the costs of ministry expenses. If a credit card system is preferred, stringent policies need to be made for the use of the card, such as forbidding use of the card for personal expenses. In addition, only one person should control a corporate card. That person then takes complete responsibility for the record keeping and security of the card. Monthly, the statement needs to be verified by the employee, marked with the correct account numbers to charge for the expenses, approved by the employee's supervisor, and given to the treasurer for prompt payment before interest must be added.

Not many employees will be able to justify carrying a corporate card in the church's name, but those doing much travel or paying for groups will appreciate its portability and convenience. With a church credit card, the employee will not have to pay for ministry expenses initially out of personal income before being reimbursed. Since credit cards offer limitless opportunity for abuse, however, staff supervision is of extreme importance.

Humorist Michael Davis deadpans: "I started out with nothing, and I still have most of it." Churches conscientious about the way they spend God's money can do Davis one better by testifying, "We started out with something, and we have practically none of it left; the rest we spent judiciously on God's work."

For Further Reading

Berkley, James D., ed. *Handbook of Management and Administration*. Grand Rapids: Baker, 1997. Chapter 37 deals with many aspects of church spending.

Busby, Daniel. *The Zondervan Church and Nonprofit Organization Tax and Financial Guide*. Grand Rapids: Zondervan, 2000. Busby always gives solid, clear, illustrated advice.

Tennyson, Mack. *Church Finances for People Who Count*. Grand Rapids: Zondervan, 1990. His words on internal control are especially good.

Seven

Planned Giving and Foundations

Two pockets are better than one. You will probably agree as you cram your ski jacket pockets with keys, money, gloves, and Kleenex. Churches discover this truth when they investigate planned giving and learn that donors have two pockets from which to give.

Churches are rather adept at digging into the pocket labeled *current income.* Pledge drives and stewardship sermons spur people to give a proportionate amount of their income. Children learn to tithe their allowance. People soon get the point that if they are earning an income, they should return a portion of it to God. That's fundamental giving out of the first pocket.

But most people boast a second pocket labeled *accumulated wealth.* In this pocket they keep their certificates of deposit, stock certificates, real estate holdings, life insurance policies, IRAs, tax-sheltered annuities, pension plans, bank and savings accounts, valuable collections, business holdings, partnerships, mutual funds, home equity, jewelry, fine art, fat wads of cash, lottery winnings, surplus vehicles, precious metals, and the cattle on several hills. (It's a big pocket.)

Many churches never consider this second pocket, a pocket growing in unprecedented ways in the last couple of decades. The Builder generation, who toughed out the Great Depression and won the Second World War, has been tenacious in building wealth. The Builder generation typically has been active in church and faithful in stewardship commitment. Look around—builders likely are the financial pillars holding up your church.

The Builder generation, however, is aging quickly, and within a decade or so, enormous amounts of accumulated wealth will go from Builder second pockets into Boomer second pockets—Boomers, who left the established church in the '60s and have only trickled back in the last three decades; Boomers, who generally lack institutional loyalty and, unlike most of their community-centered Builder parents, are me-centered.

What will become of the vast accumulated wealth of the Builders, who in their generation generally erased the label of *poor* in "poor old person" as they tooled off in their motor homes with their platinum cards in the second pocket of comfortable retirement clothes? Will the Builders' values, expressed in their lifetime, be expressed in their estates? Will their church giving be able to continue beyond their living? Or will Baby Boomers inherit all that accumulated wealth to pay off their accumulated consumer credit?

And my Boomer generation, those of us who have wandered back into faith or never left—this generation is enormous. It is now in its peak earning years. It is poised to inherit piles of wealth from parents. Boomers are on the verge of having overstuffed second pockets.

Will the church look into second pockets?

A Case for Second-Pocket Giving

Consider Will and Vera Bauer, a couple of Builders conveniently made up for this illustration. After the war and some college on the GI Bill, Will and Vera married and settled on the small family farm. Will helped his dad, and Vera was a public-health nurse. Soon, however, Vera started raising kids. She got back to nursing only after the children were all in school. Will, meanwhile, found he had a mechanical bent and moved from tinkering on the farm to starting his own small, farm-machinery business. He kept the farm, but as he got busier at the shop, he started leasing the land. The business prospered, the farm and their new home in town appreciated, and Vera's new supervisory job brought in plenty of money to save and invest. In 1985 Will and Vera sold the business and farm and retired in their paid-for home, far more financially comfortable than they had ever dreamed they would be.

Prior to 1985 the Bauers' income was close to $150,000 a year. Being good Lutherans, they tithed from that first pocket. In retirement, however, the Bauers now live on investment income, Social Security, and various pension-type proceeds. They are very comfortable on about $60,000 a year, with few major expenses. They now give $6,000 a year to church, compared to $15,000 before retirement, and their little church feels the loss.

The Bauers' personal industry and thrift, however, have produced an overflowing second pocket. Will has a $100,000 life insurance policy. Vera won't need it, and the two kids have done great, one with Microsoft and the other with nearby Gateway Computers, so they won't need it. *How about making their beloved church the beneficiary of the life insurance policy?*

There's the old Converse farm the Bauers bought years ago and held on to. It's right where the interstate is getting a new interchange, and the town is growing in that direction. That dinky old Converse spread, bought for $10,000 in 1955, is now worth $300,000. Can you believe it? Uncle Sam does, and if the Bauers sell the appreciated property, they will lose an enormous amount to capital gains taxes. *If they donate the land to their church, the Bauers can gain excellent tax benefits.*

In a like manner, each asset the Bauers control could benefit the church to which they are deeply committed. Certainly no legitimate church would want to sit down with the Bauers and methodically strip away their every asset, transferring each one to the church's control. Yet knowledgeable church representatives could work with the Bauers to help them preserve a portion of their assets to promote Christian causes. They now are in a position to benefit their church exceedingly from the second pocket, even while their faithful first-pocket donations are diminished.

The Bauers can be found in nearly every church. Surprisingly few churches, however, consider their bulging second pocket.

Win-Win Planned Giving

A fascinating aspect of much of planned giving is the mutual benefit that can be derived. The church doesn't walk away the sole beneficiary. In many cases the donor receives not only the blessed satisfaction of giving but also a tangible financial benefit, such as lowered tax liability, peace of mind, or secured income for life. The church that counsels with members about their second-pocket giving isn't "pulling a fast one."

The church is wisely providing opportunities for lasting stewardship.

Churches lag behind universities, hospitals, seminaries, foundations, and other institutions in promoting planned giving. But the church can appropriate the pioneering expertise of these groups. A number of planned-giving vehicles are being used successfully by nonprofits, such as:

- *Charitable gift annuities.* This sounds almost too good to be true. Through a charitable gift annuity, the donor can receive an immediate tax deduction and a largely tax-free permanent income, and the church receives a significant contribution. The key is that the donor transfers specific assets to the church, and the church then gives the donor a set income for life, the amount being determined by the amount of the donation and the donor's age. The donor typically receives a greater income from the charitable gift annuity than he or she would draw from investing the assets in other safe investments.

  When the donor dies, the church receives the remaining assets, averaging about half of the original gift. Through reinsuring its obligation, the church can receive immediate but lesser funds.

  Other similar financial instruments such as *remainder annuity trusts* and *remainder unitrusts* work on the same principles. Charitable gift annuities require a good measure of financial and legal sophistication, but churches and their members can benefit immeasurably from them. Legal and financial counsel is highly advised!

- *Life insurance.* Many older persons carry paid-up whole-life policies that they no longer need. When they had children or a spouse to provide for, the insurance made a lot of sense. Now, it's just another asset. Simply by naming the church the beneficiary, these persons can give a tremendous donation on their death. This, of course, means their spouse or children won't receive the benefit, but in many cases other inheritances make the life insurance unnecessary.

In the year the church is named beneficiary, the donor receives a tax deduction equal to the replacement value of the insurance policy. If the donor continues to pay insurance premiums, they too are deductible in the years in which they are paid.

- *Pooled income fund.* Through this plan a number of people donate assets to the church, and the donations are pooled. When the pooled fund earns interest, the interest is distributed to the donors. When a pool member dies, the church receives that person's share.

  As in other similar plans, the donations need to be truly given and not just in effect loaned to the church. People do transfer ownership of their assets, but with an agreement about income during their lifetime. Again, donors also receive tax benefits.

- *Appreciated assets.* If I buy something at a lower price, hold it, and sell it at a higher price, I owe taxes on the money I make from the appreciation of the assets.

  Remember the Bauers' $10,000 property that became worth $300,000? Let's say they want the church to have it. Wanting to make it simple for the church, they plan to sell it and just give the church the money. Not a good idea. After selling the property, they would have to pay taxes on

$290,000 of capital gain—at least $29,000 in taxes. Thus they could give the church no more than $271,000 and claim it as a charitable deduction.

If, instead, the Bauers simply gave the church the appreciated property, they could claim a charitable deduction of the full value—$300,000. The church could then sell the land and receive $300,000, rather than $271,000, from the Bauers.

In effect, the church gets to keep money that would be lost to taxes in the other method. What works for real estate has similar application to other tangible gifts of appreciated assets, such as art collections, stamp collections, antiques, or stocks.

- *Wills and bequests.* This is the most straightforward of the bunch. The church ought to be written into every Christian's will. If in living we want our resources to promote the kingdom of God, in death we can give a portion of our estate to perpetuate that commitment. A sizable bequest to a church makes particular sense on the death of an elderly single or widowed person, when there is no close family, or when survivors' needs are well met by other means. Even people of modest means can give a tremendous blessing as their second pocket is cleared out a final time with at least some of their estate going to their church.

Before entering into any planned-giving arrangement, church and giver need to be certain that all parties understand the ramifications of the gift. In seeking tax benefits from charitable contributions, people cannot expect to give their way to wealth. Charitable giving remains *giving*, even when tax benefits may make the true cost less than the face cost.

Leadership Gifts

Large contributions from deep-pocket donors sometimes are called *leadership gifts*. Art museums, libraries, colleges, and pastors in Texas, from my experience, know well how to handle such out-of-the-ordinary philanthropy. It can be tricky. No pastor wants to fawn over the wearers of big gold rings (James 2:1–4), and the smaller gift of a less wealthy person may in truth be a greater gift (Mark 12:41–44). But at the same time, if significant contributions of time or services warrant special attention from the pastor, so should significant contributions of wealth.

Perhaps surprisingly, discreet recognition from the pastor is often preferred over public recognition. Major givers usually appreciate acknowledgment of their gifts and the satisfaction of information about what the gift can accomplish, but many would rather not be recognized in a broadly public way for a couple of reasons. First, they don't want to herald their good deeds, preferring to be more modest. Second, they don't want a line to form at their door asking for handouts.

Churches need to decide their policy for leadership gifts. Do rooms and buildings get named after givers? Do name plaques festoon walls, furnishings, and implements? Are special funds set up, with trustees determining how the funds are used—which can lead to conflicting purposes? How many and what kinds of strings will the church allow to be attached to major donations? Many decisions must be made on a case-by-case basis, but a general policy helps pastors who find themselves with a wealthy person's arm around their shoulder and an offer they almost cannot refuse.

Noncash Gifts

Cash, we know how to receipt. But what do we do with the gift of five acres of bottomland that floods every spring? The church has decisions to make and responsibilities to fulfill.

First, the church needs to decide if it wants to accept the gift. Churches are not forced to receive gifts and are actually wise to turn down gifts they either cannot use or cannot honor. The decision may be as simple as saying no thanks to the would-be donation of a torn-arm, sprung-cushion couch for the youth room. It may be as hard as turning down tens of thousands of dollars in apparent land valuation from a shady source.

Some gifts can be wearyingly entangling. I knew a church that received as a bequest a third mortgage on a home. The current occupant defaulted on the mortgages and left town. Now three parties were left to sort out a repossession. The church ended up paying several thousand dollars in fees and back taxes and far too many hours of volunteer time over nearly three years to finally net less than $10,000 from the eventual sale of the home. The church could have just walked away from the deal.

Some so-called gifts can be horrifyingly costly. Of particular note are real estate donations of former service stations or industrial properties. Unscrupulous or unknowing "benefactors" can burden the church with sky-high environmental cleanup costs. Before receiving property, a church needs to consider the advisability of an environmental study to determine such deal killers as contaminated soil or hazardous wastes.

The church that accepts noncash gifts also takes on the responsibility of giving proper receipts to the donor and reports to the IRS. This has been made necessary by law because people have abused the deduction by donating property and overstating its value on their tax return. The value of the donation determines the receipting requirements:

- *Less than $500.* The church gives a receipt with the donor's name, the church name, the date and location of the donation, and a description of the donated property ("three grocery bags of children's clothing in good shape" or "Commodore 64 computer and monitor in working condition"). Do not, however, attach a value to the items. In fact the church should not set a value figure on any non-cash donation receipt. Donors do not need a receipt for donated property worth less than $250 but they must have it for gifts estimated at over $250.
- *$500 to $5,000.* Many more record-keeping requirements kick in for the *donor* at this point, including appraising the value of the property, telling how the appraisal was arrived at, and listing any use agreements made with the church. The donor must also send in IRS Form 8283 with the front side filled in. The church's responsibility remains the same—the receipt, with no valuation given by the church.
- *Greater than $5,000.* Now the *donor* must obtain a qualified appraiser to set the value of the donation. This is filled in on the back of Form 8283, and a church representative needs to sign that form. The church also gives the donor a receipt, as above.

A further *significant* obligation remains for the church as recipient of a noncash donation greater than $5,000. If the church sells the large gift donated to the congregation within two years of first receiving it, the church must complete and return Form 8282 to the IRS within 125 days after the sale. Form 8282 is simple and basically tells the IRS what the church received for the original donation it has now sold. The IRS, of course, compares that value to the one claimed by the original donor.

Note: If the church does not file a Form 8282, the tax return of the *donor* may be selected for examination by the IRS. In other words, if the church forgets to get around to filing Form 8282, it is doing its kind benefactor no favor!

How Firm a Foundation?

The church's one foundation is Jesus Christ her Lord. But many churches could also benefit from an altogether different foundation: a charitable foundation. Many denominations and charitable organizations have foundations to receive endowments and channel the proceeds toward specific purposes. Some larger and financially sophisticated churches enjoy the benefits of foundations as well.

Should a church seek endowments? The positive side is obvious: greater funds available to support the church's ministry. What church couldn't use multiple thousands of extra dollars a year? How exciting to be able to renovate that Christian education wing with endowment funds and leave the general fund for program purposes! Yet churches need to consider soberly the impact a foundation would have on the congregation. Negative factors include:

- *The possible siphoning of money into the foundation that might have been given to the program budget.* When a foundation is established, lots of energy, excitement, and publicity hail its arrival. Efforts to fund the foundation may cannibalize funds that would have ended up in the offering plate.

Solution: The foundation can be set up to receive mainly specific donations, such as planned-giving contributions, bequests, and gifts from entities that would not normally contribute to church operations. Education of the congregation can stress the over-and-above quality of gifts to the foundation.

- *A rogue foundation board that clashes with the church board.* This possibility has been reality more often than one would hope. When the church board is trying to move the congregation in one direction and the foundation board, characteristically more conservative or facilities focused, is dead set on heading another, ugly clashes have resulted.

  Solution: The foundation charter needs to set up the board so that it maintains a healthy measure of independence from the church board but also has both strong ties, through personnel and purpose, and similar focus, through communication and purpose statement. Rotation of board members is essential, with nominees passing muster first by the church board. When the board is allowed to become ingrown and possessive, a foundation turns troublesome.

- *Diminished incentive for church members to give.* Foundations are notorious for causing general-giving weakness among the rank and file in highly endowed churches. People think: *The foundation has millions. The church doesn't need my few thousand.*

  Solution: Foundation money should not be used to enable financial codependency by the congregation. If the foundation's big bucks are used time and again to rescue a giving-impaired congregation, the church members will be trained to sit back and let it. From the establishment of the foundation, it should have specific regulations about the spending of the funds so that endowment dollars don't displace stewardship giving. Appropriate uses of foundation funds may include capital improvements, major repairs (such as a new boiler—not maintenance calls), seed money for bold new initiatives, missions work, matching funds for special giving, facilities debt retirement, college and seminary scholarships, and denominational causes.

A well-established, scrupulously operated church charitable foundation can do a tremendous amount of good as it absorbs the proceeds of planned giving and funnels them into ministry through the life of the congregation and beyond. While this is not an activity to be entered into lightly or without excellent financial and legal counsel, churches have much to gain by investigating the possibility.

The Usual Small Print

Nearly everything contained in this chapter has legal ramifications. Tax laws change. Government regulations proliferate. New financial vehicles are dreamed up. Fallen people find new ways to make good institutions troublesome. Thus pastors and church leaders are prudent to consider this and any other financial advice as simply that—advice. They must diligently seek competent counsel by attorneys, CPAs, and financial advisors who are trained, up-to-date, and certified in this particular aspect of the law, and who do not stand to gain personally from the counsel given.

Churches, frugal as they are, may well need to pay for that counsel. Charge the foundation!

For Further Reading

Busby, Daniel. *The Zondervan Church and Nonprofit Organization Tax and Financial Guide*. Grand Rapids: Zondervan, 2000. As always, Busby presents detailed, accurate information.

Hammar, Richard. *Church and Clergy Tax Guide*. Matthews, N.C.: Christian Ministry Resources, 1997. Hammar is unsurpassed as an authority on tax matters for churches.

Tennyson, Mack. *Church Finances for People Who Count*. Grand Rapids: Zondervan, 1990. Provides helpful information on noncash gifts.

Raising Capital

Nearly every American Christian enjoys the fruits of a capital campaign or two. I am particularly taken by church architecture of the 1920s. Several of my favorite church buildings—including First Presbyterian in Yakima, Washington—were built in that era, just before the Great Depression, which made paying off the grand building projects a nightmare. But a capital campaign back in the optimistic Roaring Twenties allowed those beautiful edifices to be erected to the glory of God.

The fact is that every building in which I've worshiped had to be purchased or built at some time, in most cases following a capital campaign I neither conceived nor helped finance. Yet I still have had the pleasure of using the buildings.

Sometimes, however, the spade is in our hands at the groundbreaking, and the dollars must come from contemporary pockets, from *our* pockets. *We* get the pleasure and share the responsibility of capitalizing and realizing a church building project to pass on to future generations. This responsibility, while not for the easily daunted, has been shouldered often enough that considerable wisdom has accumulated on the subject.

To Campaign or Not to Campaign?

A *capital campaign* must remain distinct from the annual stewardship campaign, both in people's minds as a concept and in reality as a church activity. Capital campaigns, appropriately enough, raise capital—large amounts, in most instances, for designated purposes. In contrast, annual stewardship campaigns provide the regular income for church overhead and programs. Most of the work for the annual stewardship campaign (see chapter 4) has its counterpart in a capital campaign, but the purposes of the two campaigns differ, as does the use of the money raised.

The most common reason for a capital campaign is a building or remodeling project of such scope that it would drain the current budget and still not receive adequate funding. Capital improvements often require a capital campaign. But capital campaigns may be launched for other significant needs, such as the endowment of a chair at a seminary, a large-scale missions project like developing an impoverished village, debt retirement that allows the church to get out from under staggering loan repayments, or a major initiative to bring on added staff or launch a significant new program.

Whatever the purpose of the capital campaign, the number one decision remains: Should we do it? A capital campaign demands much of the church—careful thought, pastor's time, planning, meetings, programs, and seed money, not to mention the members' sacrificial giving. A capital drive cannot be undertaken lightly. It often becomes *the* activity of the year, whatever year it is kicked off.

Thus the first question to ask is, Are there any alternatives? A church probably should not mount a capital campaign if:

- *It is lacking corporate strength.* Weak, foundering congregations do not have the ability to launch a successful campaign. A capital campaign won't work to revitalize a moribund congregation. It most likely will become another failure rather than a turning point toward vitality. Conflicted churches, dwindling churches, churches experiencing leadership transition, churches with such ineffective leadership that they *ought* to have a leadership change— these are poor candidates for a successful campaign. A first task is to regain a measure of corporate vigor before attempting a capital drive, just as an influenza patient ought first to get up and walk around before attempting to run a marathon.
- *The cause is not singular and significant.* Some items need to stretch the general budget rather than trigger a capital campaign. Putting gutters on the fellowship hall roof is part of the annual budget. Putting a new slate roof on a historic building might necessitate a capital drive. Paying the staff goes into the budget; boldly adding a counseling center and staff could trigger a capital campaign.

  Probably the hardest capital campaign to mount is one caused by simple church debt: The church hasn't paid its bills and now it needs to be bailed out. Who gets excited about giving to correct past mistakes?

  Not every need should occasion a church's capital campaign. The occasional, significant, extraordinary needs that people can and ought to rally behind call for such a campaign.
- *Other means can meet the need.* As appropriate and kind as it is for a community to rally around a family burned out of their home, it would be silly to mount the same social-welfare campaign if there

had been no fire. The measure of response needs to match the level of need. If a church can use cash reserves or sell unnecessary property to build that social hall, it need not begin a financial campaign. Again, the magnitude of the response must reflect the need. Only when no other normal means would allow a given initiative—one the church has determined necessary and proper—should a capital campaign be contemplated.

- *The pastor opposes it.* A church conceivably could conduct a successful capital campaign without the pastor's enthusiastic support, but it would be a miracle. A campaign is complicated enough without adding the deleterious factor of pastoral neglect or opposition. Normally a campaign consumes enormous amounts of the pastor's time and attention. People look to the pastor for direction. The pastor's personal contribution to the campaign sometimes plays a key role. Without the pastor on board, a capital campaign is practically doomed to failure. With a pastor's hearty support, a campaign has a fighting chance to succeed.

  Any pastor needs to think twice before embarking on a capital campaign. It will not make for a calm, stress-free year. It can, however, produce tremendous spiritual and financial rewards for the congregation and ought not to be dismissed offhandedly.

- *A cause not worthy of the effort.* Sometimes churches plan a building program for the wrong reasons. The pastor may want a lasting monument to her leadership. The members may want to gold-plate their surroundings to give themselves a more comfortable "clubhouse." The church down the street is getting ahead of them. Or it may have been suggested that a building project will enliven the church.

Wouldn't it be a shame to entangle so much of the people's time, energy, and money on a project that does not bring glory to God and aid to his people? A capital campaign must have a bedrock purpose that is theologically, morally, and fiscally sound to the core.

Who Heads the Campaign?

Should the campaign be led by someone from the church or by an outside consultant? That's a major question. In most cases, churches retain a professional fund-raising consultant. The case for the consultant is strong:

- No one knows fund-raising like a pro. (But of course, that same professional smoothness may not sit well with a congregation wondering why the church leaders would turn an outsider loose on the church.)
- There is so much campaign work to do that the church pastor or staff would be strained to do it themselves and it would take them away from the tasks God has called and gifted them to do. (But even with a consultant, the requirements on the pastor and staff remain significant. The campaign simply *will* consume a great deal of time and energy.)
- Churches tend to work harder for an outside consultant, taking seriously the consultant's recommendations and laboring to have materials and programs ready when the person comes. (But not if they resent the person or question his or her necessity and cost. If a church is already a well-

oiled, businesslike machine, it may not need a hired hand to hold its feet to the fire.)

- Consultants bring knowledge from many churches and other parts of the country, equipping the congregation in ways their staff couldn't be expected to do. (But no one knows the local church like its pastor and staff, and outside ratios and theories and methods may fall flat in this particular church.)
- Church members realize the significance of the capital campaign when what amounts to another part-time employee is retained to make the program successful. (But parishioners may resent the cost and imposition of someone from outside, as if they are being "worked over" by a pro.)
- The consultant can perhaps be more "prophetic" than the already-familiar pastor. (Or a consultant can offend a church by an approach that is too hard sell.)
- The consultant obviously is at home with fund-raising and good at it, compared to the local staff, who may be uncomfortable with the role and added responsibilities. (But in any given church, the pastor or a person already on staff may be highly gifted in fund-raising.)

In a like manner, a case can also be made against hiring a consultant:

- The consultant will consume some of the money raised in the campaign. They don't come cheap. (But a consultant normally helps the church discover and receive up to twice as much money on the average as the church would have received had it not used a consultant. And what is the current pastor's time worth—time that would be spent on the campaign?)

- The consultant may come from a church culture different from the congregation, and the personality clash can cause problems. (But there are so many consultants available, a wise church can retain a consultant using the same criteria it would use to call a short-term associate pastor. By searching for a consultant in the same way, a good match can be made.)
- The decision can appear extravagant: "Why hire someone to twist our arms for more money, when what we really need is a youth pastor?" (But some people will choose whatever reason seems convenient to oppose a capital campaign. A well-chosen consultant can, in a few months, lay the foundation for a stronger church for years to come, one eventually capable of hiring that youth pastor.)
- Church leaders already know how to conduct a campaign without hiring someone from the outside. This may be the case in some instances, especially for churches with repeat campaigns. I know of one church beginning its fourth three-year campaign in a row. For the first three, they enjoyed the benefits of a consultant, but for the fourth campaign, they chose to use their experience and merely confer with a consultant. (But the capital-campaign world is constantly changing, and the success of previous consultant-led campaigns may not be a fluke. Is it worth it to break the pattern and possibly break the record of success?)

The bottom line? Yes, most churches choose to hire a consultant, and very few regret it. A capital campaign is simply too vital and complicated an enterprise to undertake without someone qualified to show the way.

Choice Considerations

In choosing a professional to work with the church, it's good to remember the difference between a *fund-raiser* and a *fund-raising consultant*. A *fund-raiser* typically makes the calls on potential donors and solicits contributions, often using a personality and technique honed over years to be effective. A *fund-raising consultant* helps train and equip the church to do their own fund-raising; this person or her professional team does not call on potential donors.

This is a major distinction, and much counsel strongly favors retaining a fund-raising consultant. Fund-raisers may sound good, in that they appear to do most of the work for the church. Their methods, however, too easily can be perceived as too slick, too pushy, or too foreign to a given church. They can alienate potential givers or cause hard feelings. Also the church itself misses out on the opportunity to mobilize a broad army of support for the purpose of the capital campaign.

Another nearly universal piece of counsel is to avoid agreements with fund-raising consultants that guarantee a percentage of the income to the consultant. Again, on the surface, a percentage basis could appear to be a fine motivator for the consultant, guaranteeing the person's attention and conscientious efforts. But practice has proven the percentage idea to be fraught with difficulties: It promotes overzealousness and arm-twisting, it confuses motivations, it can lead to inflated expectations or even tax complications, and it may overcompensate the consultant if the church is especially generous in its giving. A straight, up-front consulting fee is a much preferred way of operating.

The Course of a Campaign

While each campaign is unique and consultants operate differently, certain activities characterize most capital campaigns. Campaigns usually begin with what should be a free consultation with the fund-raising consultant. The consultant's plan is to get to know the church, analyze the possibilities, and present a giving estimate, a campaign plan, and a fixed fee to the church leaders. The church, on the other hand, wants to size up the potential of the consultant and see if the style, personality, and program match is good.

Because the consultant may expend a fair amount of time and expense to meet with the church, the church leaders should do their homework first and invite only a small number of the most promising consultants to meet with them—say, two or three. Prior screening can be done using printed materials, phone interviews, and reference checks. Once the choice is made, an agreement is usually signed.

To join the pastor and church staff, most churches recruit a sizable team of volunteers, with the advice of the consultant. Many people are needed to fill such roles as cochairs of the campaign, publicity committee members, prayer team members, special-event coordinators, hosts and hostesses for dinners or coffees, visitation team members, follow-up committee members, leadership-giving chairpersons, phone teams, people to arrange testimonials, commitment teams, and any number of other roles. Team members usually are given job descriptions, materials, and training by the consultant.

One key to a successful campaign is the involvement of a large number of people, each of whom brings friends, relatives, and coworkers into the planning process. When the actual campaign unfolds, many people have already bought into the idea. By this time they have contributed time and effort to the process, and others have confidence in the enterprise because they have seen friends happily wrapped up in the effort.

Campaign leaders often choose a theme or slogan to get the campaign purpose into people's thoughts, something like "A Time to Build" or "Continuing the Vision." Sometimes a hymn or chorus becomes a theme song. Attractive printed materials translate the abstract need into concrete images to capture people's interest. People have a hard time just throwing money into an accumulated pile, but if they know their sacrificial giving will produce a new preschool wing and buy a truck for the peasant farmers in Guatemala, they can begin to get excited about that.

Churches today often produce a campaign video, have an architect create a model of the new church building, mail full-color brochures about the project, or even create a Web page with all the details. The goal is to get the vision into people's minds and hearts in a number of ways so that the need and the solution provided by the capital campaign are universally understood.

Sermons, mailed brochures, explanations during worship, testimonies, newsletter articles, informational meetings, posters and displays in the narthex, word of mouth—a few weeks of activities such as these usually lead up to a special occasion that provides an opportunity for people to pledge to what is typically a three-year commitment. The special occasion may be a big banquet with an enormous amount of energy expended toward getting people to attend. It may be a special worship service in which all the stops are pulled to make it upbeat and memorable.

Sometimes it is more of a rally, with music, testimony, and a speaker leading people to join in a commitment to the project. Sometimes it is a series of home meetings in which people gather in the homes of their friends or by neighborhood. In each case, a specific time and place is given to receive people's pledge commitments. For a day to a week or so, the focus is on commitment and on prayerfully filling out and turning in capital campaign pledge cards.

Prior to the commitment period, leadership gifts are often solicited from persons able to give sizable amounts. Through personal contacts and special meetings, these gifts are requested from the big givers. The idea is for their early pledges to be in hand so that when the big commitment period arrives, campaign leaders can announce that a large portion of the goal has already been met through the leadership gifts. Sometimes more than half the goal is underwritten by these leadership pledges, providing encouragement to the rank-and-file givers and a sense of momentum.

Sometimes canvassing teams visit everyone in their homes, or, alternatively, contact those who hadn't pledged during the big commitment event. This personal attention can be either helpful or troublesome. It is helpful for the parties who appreciate the personal touch and want to discuss the campaign with a fellow church member. The personal call may stimulate pledges that never would be received through mass means.

Such canvassing calls can be problematic, however, for persons who have felt isolated from the church and receive their only contact when someone calls to ask them for money, or for cocooners who resent the intrusion at home, or for those who prefer not to go on record as being opposed to the campaign but are forced to when someone arrives at their door.

Some follow-up after the commitment period is usually a good idea, however, even if it is not a personal call. Phone calls may feel less intrusive for some. A follow-up letter may harvest pledges from a few people who were gone or absentminded when the commitment event debuted. Other people simply need more time or another set of the materials to replace those they've misplaced. Often it is these final few pledges rounded up late in the game that determine if a goal is met and the campaign is successful.

The campaign usually draws to a close with some kind of "victory day" that celebrates what the people have pledged. A final pledge figure is announced. The people hear what their giving will accomplish. They are congratulated and thanked by the campaign leadership, and the people in turn recognize the untiring efforts of the campaign volunteers. God is thanked for his gracious work and invoked to bless the results. It is a fitting conclusion to what has been a vigorous period in the life of the church.

Typically people who pledge are given special envelopes to use to keep the capital-campaign gifts separate from their regular offering. Throughout the three-year pay-up period, it is always a good idea to keep people posted on both their pay up on their pledge and on the progress of the project their pledge is funding. After the capital-campaign blitz, it is easy for leaders to rest on their laurels. But three years is a long time, and people greatly appreciate seeing the effects their giving is having. Pay-up percentages remain much higher in churches that carefully follow up the pledgers throughout the pledge period. Pay-up rates of 90 to 98 percent aren't uncommon in such cases.

Borrowing through Bonds

Some churches borrow money to buy land or to build through issuing bonds. This is a somewhat complicated process that demands professional counsel. Laws vary by state and change within states, but most jurisdictions require that bonds be issued only through licensed organizations. Thus a church cannot set itself up to issue bonds but must do it through an underwriting firm or investment banking firm, which, of course, receives payment for its services.

When a church sells bonds, it is promising to pay interest on the borrowed money and repay the principal after a specified period. The bonds usually have graduated maturity dates, so that some are paid off each year over a period of time. Often bonds are sold primarily to church members and friends, people who have an interest in the welfare of the congregation and want it to succeed. But since bonds can be a reasonably secure and beneficial form of general investment, the bonds may also be sold on the open market, where anyone can invest in them as they would in the stock market. Thus both church members and people at large can purchase the bonds that allow the church to grow.

One potential benefit of bonds is that they may be donated back to the church by those who buy them with that intention, rather than having them paid off. A church member may enjoy the income from the investment, but when the bond matures and is to be redeemed, the member simply gives it up as a donation. Thus the church doesn't have to pay off that portion of its debt. Those who purchase the bonds have every right to be repaid on maturity of their bonds and should never be made to feel cheap if they choose to redeem their bonds. However, many churches have experienced a high rate of donation of matured bonds when the opportunity is given to the owners who are members.

Bonds are set up in a way that the church can *call* them before maturity at given dates, allowing the congregation to pay off the bondholders even before the bonds are due. If the church is able to get a better interest rate through another form of borrowing after a few years or if it has the funds to pay off its debt and forgo interest expenses altogether, calling the bonds early allows the church to do so. Those bondholders depending on the interest income from the bonds may be disappointed to have their bonds called early, so such an eventuality should be made clear to the purchasers from the time of selling the bonds.

Chaplain Ben Patterson of Hope College tells the story in *Leadership* journal of a mother who found her young son crying one morning as he was tying his shoes. "Why are you crying?" she asked.

"I have to tie my shoes," he sobbed.

"But you just learned how. It isn't *that* hard, is it?"

"But I'm gonna have to do it the rest of my life!" he wailed.[1]

For church leaders, raising capital may seem like tying one's shoes for a little boy—an endless, onerous task. Actually, it isn't—endless, that is. Some day you will retire.

For Further Reading

Berkley, James D., ed. *Handbook of Management and Administration*. Grand Rapids: Baker, 1997. Chapter 34 has a number of useful articles.

Bowman, Ray, and Eddy Hall. *When Not to Build*. Rev. ed. Grand Rapids: Baker, 2000. A wise contrarian's counsel that needs to be read before embarking on a building project.

Chaffee, Paul. *Accountable Leadership: Resources for Worshipping Communities*. San Francisco: ChurchCare Publishing, 1993. Chaffee has a strong section on fund-raising, including a code of ethics.

Miller, Kevin A. "Fund-raising Consultants: Getting the Pros, Not the Con." *Leadership* (winter 1987): 92. A comprehensive, excellent article on fund-raising for churches.

Legal and Tax Matters

Early in 1999 the Associated Press carried a story by Curt Anderson about the IRS: "It sounds like a taxpayer's dream: The IRS was audited and struggled to explain its own financial records." Yes, the congressional General Accounting Office audited the tax auditors, and the IRS came up lacking. "The GAO found the IRS did a good job of collecting $1.8 trillion in tax revenue in fiscal 1998," Anderson continues. "The main problems were found in the agency's administration of an $8.1 billion annual budget."[1] In other words, the IRS got our money; they just couldn't manage theirs particularly well.

Churches dare not be found likewise wanting in tax and other legal matters, for unlike the IRS, the church *does* have the IRS looking over its shoulder.

Staying Tax-Exempt

A tax exemption is a terrible thing to lose. Without the exemption, the church must pay taxes, members lose their charitable-donations deduction for their gifts to the church, postal rates for bulk mailings go up, participation in 403(b) annuities is lost, and the church's favored status to receive philanthropic funding disappears.

Churches should be exempt from federal taxation under Section 501(c)(3) of the Internal Revenue Code. This section is the religious institution's good friend and benefactor, for it cuts churches even more slack than it does for other exempt organizations, such as scientific, educational, and charitable groups.

In most states and other jurisdictions, likewise, laws make most churches *nonprofit* or *not-for-profit* organizations. Again, this shields churches from having to pay many of the taxes individuals and businesses must pay, such as property tax, income tax, and, in some states, even sales tax.

Of course, with any such benefit—which can be substantial—abuses have occurred. Individuals wanting to shelter their income from taxation have unilaterally declared themselves to be churches. Businesses have tried to incorporate as churches to be tax-exempt. Churches have sometimes entered the business world with operations in competition with legitimate businesses that have to pay taxes, and that competition has been unfair to the businesses.

Thus, regulations have been sharpened to curtail such abuse. Churches are wise to stay well within certain *safe harbors* to not risk losing the benefit of tax exemption. A couple of practices are advised:

Substantiating the Church's Exempt Status

Unless one's "church" is really a front for Cousin Guido's Taxi Service, it is probably exempt under federal law. Factors such as having a regular worship service, a distinct religious history, an established place of worship, and a formal code of doctrine and discipline delineate a legitimate church.

For state and local jurisdictions, however, nonprofit status becomes more tenuous. Some require regular filing of forms and updating of credentials. Thus a church once exempt may not always be exempt, especially if a form isn't filed in a timely manner. Some jurisdictions exempt the church from one form of taxation—say, property—while charging for another, such as sales tax. Some exempt only a portion of the property or fight tenaciously with the church over what is necessary for religious use and what should be taxed.

Each congregation ought to have some officer or employee responsible for maintaining its current state and local not-for-profit status. In addition, in places where the church is exempt from sales tax, those who make church purchases should be equipped with the church's exemption number. Church purchases made free of sales tax are like getting a discount of several percentage points.

Refraining from Support of Political Candidates

Tax-exempt organizations cannot use their funds to further the political aspirations of candidates for office. While churches can take stands for or against *issues* at election times, they cannot endorse, promote, fund, or repudiate specific *candidates.*

Churches have gained increased IRS scrutiny or had to fight for their exempt status by such actions as funding a newspaper advertisement in opposition to a presidential candidate, donating to a candidate's reelection campaign, having a local candidate address the congregation during a campaign, or publishing a voters' guide to the candidates that even appears to be politically or ideologically slanted in any way.

Spreading the Good Around

Why does the government offer such a great deal to churches—this tax exemption? The government recognizes the massive amount of good churches provide to the common social welfare. The stability, moral fiber, acts of charity, and other services churches routinely provide a community strengthen that community. Thus it is in the state's interest to encourage such activities, which it does through the tax exemption. In a secular sense, it is not unlike giving an industry tax incentives to locate a manufacturing plant in the community, where it will bring jobs and community benefits.

The state does not, however, want that benefit to end up in the pockets of individuals rather than the community at large. If a church is to be tax-exempt, the subsequent good it can do is intended for the community, not the private benefit of individuals. Thus the government keeps a wary eye on nonprofits to be sure the money they save in taxes gets distributed widely in services and doesn't instead enrich shrewd, well-placed individuals.

A for-profit organization can pay its executives and workers pretty much whatever the market will bear. As long as the organization reports salaries to the government, the government cares relatively little about the amounts.

Not so with nonprofits, including churches. Those who lead and work for churches must be paid modestly; they must not profit unduly from public concessions meant to be distributed for the common good. They can be paid, certainly; they just can't be made rich.

The technical term used for this unwelcome funneling of community good into an individual's pockets is *inurement of private benefit*. Benefits meant for the whole should not inure to private individuals. A not-for-profit can actually make a "profit"—it can spend less than it takes in in a given period—but it cannot turn those "profits" into exceedingly large benefits for any individuals associated with the organization. Thus the company you found can make you rich; the church you found shouldn't.

Churches can get into inurement-of-private-benefit trouble in a number of ways, such as:

- *Paying any employee an unreasonably large salary.* When lifestyles become grand and opulent from money made by an employee of a nonprofit, something is wrong. There is no specific figure for how much is too much to pay a pastor, but pastors making twice to three times or more what their peers make would be vulnerable to charges. It is safer to be within the pack in salary surveys than way out ahead of persons in comparable positions.

- *Giving the manse to a beloved retiring pastor.* A church may want to show deep appreciation for decades of service, but giving an officer of the church property meant for group benefit is likely a mistake. It represents too great of a corporate benefit being transferred into private hands.

- *Making sweetheart loans to church officers or employees.* This gets tricky, since churches often participate in a form of equity sharing to make it possible for pastors to buy a home in the community. What a church cannot do is give the pastor outright a benefit or compensation that is too lavish for the work rendered. Nor can resources of the organization be transferred to a private individual if they are greater than customary pay for the position.

In some states, any loan from a nonprofit to an officer or employee is forbidden. Even in those states where such loans are possible, any amount that the loan betters the going rate in the community is considered to be taxable income to the employee. In other words, if the loan is at 3 percent interest and the going rate is 8 percent, the pastor must pay taxes on the interest-payment savings. The same is true whenever a church forgives a loan to an employee—another practice fraught with inurement implications.

- *Approving under-the-table deals with church officers or employees.* Conflict-of-interest problems arise when someone in a leadership position in a not-for-profit organization stands to gain in a business deal. It is all right for an elder to sell the church medical insurance at going rates for its employees, but it is not kosher for that elder to make a special deal because of his position that provides him excessive profit at the church's loss. The church's resources should not be transferred to his private benefit—or anyone else's—because of an insider relationship.

- *Entering into business deals or practices that don't further the exempt organization's purposes.* The whole board could tour Disney World at church expense, but does that further the organization's purposes? Junkets for leaders, expensive leased cars, lavish retreats, sales of church property at less than its value, use of the church database to further a trustee's Ponzi scheme—these are the kind of suspect activities that point to inurement of private benefit and can get the church and the parties involved in hot water.

Taxing the Exempt

So that churches and other nonprofits do not compete unfairly with their business neighbors in secular trade, the federal government has instituted a tax called the Unrelated Business Income Tax (UBIT) for exempt organizations. Say your church makes really good doughnuts for the fellowship hour, and people think it would be great to sell them to raise money for missions. The church sets up a doughnut stand in the parking lot, hires some of the college students for staff, and sells doughnuts to cops and taxi drivers. They can underprice the Dunkin' Donuts place a block away because the church stand doesn't pay taxes.

Unfair, isn't it? It's also not permissible.

If the church embarks in a business, the proceeds of that business will likely be subject to UBIT if:

- *The business is unrelated to the church's tax-exempt purpose.* It's considered unrelated if it doesn't fulfill a central function of the ministry, like teaching, preaching, visiting the sick, nurturing the saints. Even if all the proceeds go to pay for bona fide church activities, simply supplying income to the organization does not make the activity substantially related. The church was exempted in order to be a *church*, not to sell doughnuts profitably.
- *The business is operated on a regular basis.* A Saturday youth car wash in the parking lot is different than opening an Auto-Bapto Car Wash that operates

like a business year-round. Intermittent bake sales or service auctions don't count for UBIT; they don't occur on a regular basis.

- *The business uses paid workers.* If the church book table blossoms into a church bookstore with paid workers, UBIT may be necessary. Other examples are operations such as a successful food service that sells to the public or a music group that turns professional and tours. A rummage sale staffed with volunteer workers wouldn't cause UBIT problems.
- *The business sells items* not *donated.* Rummage sales, bake sales, and service auctions all sell donated items—no UBIT.
- *The business earns $1,000 or more annually in gross income.* If the other factors would point toward UBIT being necessary but gross sales are below $1,000, it's still not necessary. But if in a year's time the enterprise sells goods or services totaling more than $1,000, paying UBIT probably is necessary.

Any church renting facilities to an organization which, itself, is not an exempt organization under Section 501(c)(3) will probably need to pay UBIT on the income so derived. UBIT is paid yearly using the corporate tax rate by reporting income on IRS Form 990-T.

One final caution: A great deal of UBIT activity may jeopardize a church's exempt status. If it looks like the church is in reality a business operation with a little religion tacked on for camouflage, it may be classified as such. One well-known Southern California church flirted with losing its tax-exempt status because of the number of income-producing conferences it held and the multiple extravaganzas booked into its unique sanctuary. The church that becomes a business and entertainment hub has probably ceased to be a church at heart, and the IRS is alert to smell it.

With all this said, the typical church, going about its normal churchly business, is probably not going to cause alarms to go off in IRS offices. The IRS is actually pretty cautious about taking on churches. It doesn't like to get into decisions about what is and isn't a legitimate church activity. It has little to gain by appearing to bully Christian organizations. The IRS is loath to audit a church.

By sticking with the genuine, historic work of the church, by refraining from outlandish salaries or transfers of church assets to its officers or staff, by not pushing the boundary between church and business enterprise, the vast majority of congregations quietly remain out of the IRS audit spotlight while they go about their kingdom business.

For Further Reading

Bloss, Julie. *The Church Guide to Employment Law.* Matthews, N.C.: Christian Ministry Resources, 1993. This book helps employers steer clear of legal land mines in employment issues.

Busby, Daniel. *The Zondervan Church and Nonprofit Organization Tax and Financial Guide.* Grand Rapids: Zondervan, 2000. An excellent section on UBIT.

Hammar, Richard. *Church and Clergy Tax Guide.* Matthews, N.C.: Christian Ministry Resources, 2001. This guide is updated yearly.

———. *Pastor, Church and Law.* 2d ed. Matthews, N.C.: Christian Ministry Resources, 1991. This thick volume is authoritative for legal reference.

Conclusion

It's all pretty simple in the final analysis. Church leaders conscientiously handle God's money simply to accomplish something much more important: the glory of God and the salvation, nurture, and care of souls. It is when the church forgets that money is the means to ministry that problems arise, when the church gets greedy or cute with money.

I am amused by a newspaper story that came out of Arles, France, in 1995. A bright man name André-François Raffray cooked up a grand scheme to get an apartment he wanted. In the 1960s he entered into what looked like a great deal with a 90-year-old woman: He would pay her about $500 every month until she died, and at her death, he would have the right to move into her choice apartment in this town that was once home to Vincent van Gogh.

Over the next 30 years, Raffray coughed up more than $184,000 in monthly payments for the apartment, but he never got to occupy that flat. *Raffray* died at 77 years of age around Christmas 1995, but on that day the apartment's owner, Jeanne Calment—who by then happened to be the world's oldest person at 120—feasted on foie gras and chocolate cake. And even though Raffray died, Calment would continue by law to receive her $500 a month from Raffray's heirs until her death.

I love Jeanne Calment's wry take on the whole business: "In life, one sometimes makes bad deals."[1]

Wheeling and dealing, shrewd schemes, big deals—what have these to do with the gospel? "Blessed are the *poor* in spirit," Jesus exclaimed, "for *theirs* is the kingdom of heaven" (Matt. 5:3, emphasis mine)! Prayerful, thoughtful, prudent management as a steward of God's assets—that's the church leader's fiscal responsibility.

Notes

Chapter 1: A Brief Theology of Stewardship

1. Calvin Miller, *The Finale,* quoted in *Leadership* 4, no. 4 (fall 1983): 85.
2. Gordon Cosby, *Letters to Scattered Pilgrims,* quoted in "Parables, etc." 3, no. 6 (August 1983): 1.
3. Howard L. Dayton Jr., *Leadership* 2, no. 2 (spring 1981): 62.
4. Fred Smith Sr., *Leadership* 4, no. 1 (winter 1983): 58.

Chapter 2: Prudent Practices

1. Richard Hammar, *Pastor, Church, and Law,* 2d ed. (Matthews, N.C.: Christian Ministry Resources, 1991), 336.
2. Ibid., 275.

Chapter 8: Raising Capital

1. Ben Patterson, "How to Feel Good about Your Stewardship Campaign," *Leadership* 2, no. 2 (spring 1981): 105.

Chapter 9: Legal and Tax Matters

1. Curt Anderson, *Peninsula Daily News* (Port Angeles, Wash.), 2 March 1999, p. A1.

Conclusion

1. *Bend (Oregon) Bulletin,* 12 December 1995.

Index

James D. Berkley, with three decades of ministry experience, is senior associate pastor of the First Presbyterian Church of Bellevue, Washington. He is editor of Presbyterians for Renewal's *reNEWS* and has served as editor of *Your Church* magazine and senior associate editor of *Leadership* journal. Berkley has authored and edited a number of books on pastoral practice, including the three-volume Leadership Handbooks series.

3580623

Made in the USA